TRUE CRIMES

TRUE CRIMES

chilling accounts of evil in our time

ROBERT JACKSON

SMITHMARK

A QUINTET BOOK

First published in the United States
by SMITHMARK Publishers Inc.
112 Madison Avenue, New York, NY 10016.

SMITHMARK books are available for bulk
purchase for sales promotion and premium use.
For details write or telephone the Manager of
Special Sales
SMITHMARK Publishers Inc.
112 Madison Avenue, New York, NY 10016
(212) 532-6600.

ISBN 0-8317-8671-X

This book was designed and produced by
Quintet Publishing Limited
6 Blundell Street
London N7 9BH

Creative Director: Richard Dewing
Designer: Stuart Walden
Project Editor: Damian Thompson
Editor: Robert Stewart
Picture Researcher: Liz Eddison

Typeset in Great Britain by
Central Southern Typesetters, Eastbourne
Manufactured in Hong Kong by
Regent Publishing Services Limited
Printed in Hong Kong by
Leefung-Asco Printers Limited

CONTENTS

HAW-HAW TO
BE RE-BURIED
IN EIRE

MURDER BY NUMBERS

The serial-killer and the mass-murderer are separate breeds. The one stalks his prey, year after year, planning his murders and executing them with neither pity nor passion. The other suddenly unleashes pent-up anger and frustration in an uncontrollable explosion of violence. Both have hit the headlines with alarming frequency.

THE ELUSIVE THEODORE BUNDY

LEFT
This photograph of Ted Bundy, all smiles, was taken shortly after the killer was recaptured after jumping custody in Aspen, Colorado.

For the people of Seattle, Washington, January, 1974, was the month when fear began to stalk the streets.

It started with the disappearance of Lynda Ann Healy, a student at Seattle's University of Washington. By the end of May, the total of mysterious disappearances had risen to five. All the girls were students in the Seattle area; all were attractive, with hair of at least shoulder-length; and all were aged between 18 and 22.

In the next two months three more young women vanished from the American North West, all but one of them students. By the middle of August, 1974, the tally of young women, either missing or found dead, stood at 68.

A Man Called Ted

Detectives in Washington's King County had little to go on. They knew only that one of the missing women – 23-year-old Janice Ott – had been seen in the company of a young man who called himself Ted. Four skeletons were found on Taylor Mountain, southeast of Seattle, on 1 March, 1975. They were identified by dental records; one belonged to Lynda Ann Healy.

The police had a list of more than 2,500 suspects, but the mysterious "Ted" remained elusive, as did the Volkswagen car he had reportedly been driving. By August, 1975, the list had been reduced to 94.

The victims

Bundy was sentenced to death for the murder of 12-year-old Kimberly Leach (right), but he also received separate death sentences in Florida for the killings of Margaret Bowman

and Lisa Levy (left) in 1978. There is much circumstantial evidence, however, that Bundy was responsible for many more murders — perhaps over 30. Melissa Smith, Laura

Aime, Debra Kent and Caryn Campbell are just four of the victims mentioned in this account, whose deaths bear all the hallmarks of Bundy's cruelty.

Then came the breakthrough. Robert Keppel and Roger Dunn, detectives on the case, received a telephone call from a police officer in Salt Lake City, Utah. The officer, Jerry Thompson, had spoken to a police-woman who was helping with the elimination of suspects. She had asked Thompson for information on a man called Theodore Bundy. Thompson came up with startling news. Bundy had just been arrested by the Salt Lake City police.

In October, 1974, just as the disappearances in the Seattle area ended, a similar reign of terror had begun in Salt Lake City.

Then came the breakthrough

The killings started with 17-year-old Melissa Smith, whose naked body was found in a wooded mountain area about 25 miles from the city. She had been sexually molested and strangled with a stocking. A month later, a second body, that of Laura Aime of Salem, was found on the banks of the American Fork River. Also 17 years old, Laura Aime had been raped and strangled and she had suffered a fractured skull. A third 17-year-old, Debra Kent of Bountiful, Utah, had apparently been abducted from her car. No trace of her had been found, but police had discovered a clue: a single handcuff key, lying near the spot where she had vanished.

Another woman, Carol DaRonch, told police that a man had tried to abduct her. He had fled, dropping a pair of handcuffs, when a passing motorist appeared. The key fitted them. Miss DaRonch provided a full description of the man, adding that he had been driving a light-coloured Volkswagen.

The description matched that of Theodore Bundy, arrested by the Salt Lake City police after a patrolman had seen him loitering suspiciously in a residential area in the early hours of the morning. When the officer searched Bundy's car, he made a surprising discovery: a bag containing gloves, a crowbar, an icepick, a stocking with nose and eye holes cut in it – and a pair of handcuffs.

Maps, Brochures and Credit Cards

The police searched Bundy's flat in Utah, where he was a second-year law student. He had moved there from Seattle in September, 1974. The move coincided with the start of the murders in Salt Lake City. On searching his flat, police found a Colorado road map and several brochures. One of them was a visitor's guide to Bountiful, Utah – where Debra Kent had disappeared. A second brochure featured Colorado's prominent ski

ABOVE
Theodore Bundy pictured at his trial in Miami Court, 1979. The manhunt for the killer was one of the largest in American history. No one knows to this day just how many young women Bundy murdered.

LEFT
Serial-killer Ted Bundy seen in happier days helping Carol Bartholomew, a resident of Salt Lake City, Utah, with the dishes after a birthday party. Carol remembered Bundy as a polite and attractive man.

There was no doubt where they came from. They belonged to Caryn Campbell and Melissa Smith. Even so, the evidence was not sufficient to charge Bundy with murder. However, on 23 February, 1976, Bundy appeared before the presiding judge in Salt Lake City to stand trial on the aggravated kidnap charge.

Bundy was found guilty, and sentenced to between one and fifteen years in prison. The police continued to assemble evidence against him. In October, 1976, the dossier was complete, and a warrant was issued for Bundy's arrest for the first-degree murder of Caryn Campbell.

Breaking Out

The trial began in Aspen, Colorado, on 30 December, 1977. That night, Bundy removed a light-fitting from the ceiling of his cell, climbed through the hole, and crawled along until he was above the prison warder's flat. When he heard the warder leave, he broke through the ceiling, dropped inside and walked straight through the front door into the street.

The days that followed were charged with tension. It was like sitting on a powder keg, the fuse lit. The keg exploded in the early

BELOW
Theodore Bundy's mother Louise and his stepfather John show their emotions as Judge Edward Cowart imposes the death sentence on Bundy for the murders of the two Florida State University students.

resorts, some of which had been ticked. Bundy denied ever having been to Colorado. The map and brochure, he said, had belonged to an acquaintance.

Jerry Thompson knew that there had been mysterious disappearances in Colorado, too, and he contacted colleagues there. One stood out: that of 23-year-old Caryn Campbell, who had vanished from the Wildwood Inn at Snowmass. It was one of the places ticked on Bundy's brochure. Further investigation revealed that Bundy had several times paid for petrol in Colorado by credit card. His statement that he had never visited the state was a lie.

On 1 October, 1974, the Salt Lake City police arranged an identity parade before three witnesses: Carol DaRonch and two others who had seen Bundy in Bountiful, Utah. Eight men paraded before them and the three witnesses unanimously picked out Theodore Bundy.

While Bundy was held in custody on charges of aggravated kidnapping and attempted homicide – he had tried to attack Carol DaRonch with a crowbar before she escaped – experts made a minute search of material removed from his Volkswagen. They found two samples of human hair.

ABOVE
Theodore Bundy holds his hands to his face as he makes his final statement to the court. At times, Bundy showed emotion during his statement, after which the judge sentenced him to death in the electric chair. The killer's attorney, Margaret Good, stands next to him.

hours of 15 January, 1978. In one of the halls of residence at Florida State University, Tallahassee, two young women were beaten to death. Two others were also beaten, and one raped. Elsewhere, a fifth student had been sexually molested and beaten as she lay in bed. The body of one of the dead victims, Lisa Levy, showed savage bite marks. These were photographed so that they could be matched with the teeth of suspects.

Meanwhile, police were investigating other recent disappearances. One involved a 12-year-old schoolgirl named Kimberly Leach, from Lake City, Florida, who had vanished on 9 February. A day earlier, a man driving a stolen white van had tried to abduct a young girl in Jacksonville. A few days later the van was found abandoned. It was removed for forensic examination.

On 15 February a police patrolman arrested a suspect in Pensacola. The suspect had been driving a yellow Volkswagen and behaving in a suspicious manner. The man put up a fierce struggle before being overpowered and was charged with assaulting a police officer. After two days' interrogation the suspect admitted he was Ted Bundy.

The Clinching Evidence

By this time the forensic examination of Bundy's van was beginning to pay dividends. From soil and leaves found in the vehicle experts determined that the vehicle had been in a particular area of northern

WHAT FORMS THE VIOLENT CRIMINAL – "NATURE" OR "NURTURE"?

After years of research, scientists in the United States believe that they may have isolated some of the factors that drive people to commit horrific murders. They have found that highly aggressive people have unusually high levels of the male hormone, testosterone, and low levels of the chemical, serotonin, which prevents the release of aggression by flashing "calm down" signals to the brain.

Research has established that children who are aggressive in infancy are likely to be aggressive adults. Their children, in turn, are apt to develop aggressive behaviour. One study of violent patients by the neurologist, Frank Elliott, of the University of Pennsylvania, found that 94 subjects out of 132 had a family history of violence. In some cases, violence could be traced back as far as four generations.

Medical conditions such as brain tumours can sometimes be responsible for savage crimes. Charles Whitman, who in the 1960s climbed to the top of a tower in Austin, Texas, and killed 17 passers-by before he was shot by police, had displayed a striking behavioural change in the months before the incident. A post-mortem showed that he had a brain tumour.

In another instance, a man tried to decapitate his wife and daughter with a meat cleaver. Doctors found that he had a tumour underneath the right frontal lobe. The tumour was removed and the man's behaviour reverted to normal.

identical to those in Bundy's blazer. Meanwhile, scientists had come up with vital evidence: the bite marks on Lisa Levy's body exactly matched an impression of Bundy's teeth.

No more evidence was needed. On 20 July, 1978, Bundy was charged with the first-degree murder of Kimberly Leach. A week later he was charged with the double murder in Tallahassee, and it was to stand trial on this charge that he appeared in court on 25 June, 1979. On 31 July Judge Edward Cowart sentenced Bundy to death on the count of first-degree murder.

Bundy then had to face a second trial, for the murder of Kimberly Leach. It opened in Orlando, Florida, on 7 January, 1980. When it closed a month later, Bundy was

The bite marks on Lisa Levy's body matched Bundy's teeth

found guilty of first-degree murder and kidnapping. He again received the death sentence.

Bundy launched a series of appeals and languished on Florida State Prison's death row until 1989, when the last of his appeals was dismissed and he went to his death.

How many women Theodore Bundy murdered will never be known. The number is at least 30, and may be more than 100. Bundy took that last mystery of his gruesome campaign of terror to the grave.

Florida – Suwannee State Park. There, on 7 April, searchers found the remains of Kimberly Leach, lying in an abandoned pigsty. Investigation revealed that fibres found on Kimberly Leach's clothing matched those from the carpet of the abandoned van and that bloodstains in the vehicle matched the dead girl's blood group. This in itself did not prove that Bundy had been in the van. It was not until police obtained a warrant to seize articles of Bundy's clothing that the forensic scientists finally scooped the jackpot. Some fibres found on Kimberly Leach's jeans were

THE "BOSTON STRANGLER": AN UNRESOLVED CASE

Probably the most infamous serial killer was the so-called Boston Strangler, who between June, 1962, and January, 1964, raped and strangled 13 women. His technique was to talk his way into the confidence of women living alone. When they admitted him into their homes, he raped and strangled them. His gruesome hallmark was to tie a ligature around their necks with a bow under the chin.

In June, 1962, the son of a 55-year-old divorcee, Anna Slesers, found his mother's naked body sprawled on the floor of her apartment. She had been sexually assaulted and strangled with the cord of her dressing gown. She was the Strangler's first victim.

As murder followed murder, the women of Boston were plunged into a state of terror. They barricaded themselves behind locked doors; sales of security systems rocketed. Sometimes the Strangler would take money and jewellery from his victims, apparently as a blind to make police think that robbery was the motive. Time and again, detectives

BELOW
Albert DeSalvo, the most notorious serial killer of all and the one who apparently started the murderous trend. He wormed his way into the confidence of women who lived alone, then raped and strangled them in their homes.

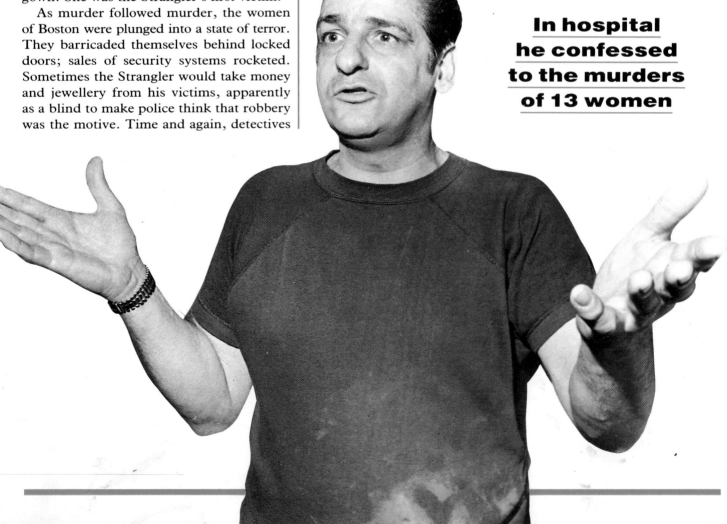

followed what seemed to be a promising lead, only to arrive at a dead end. Their work was complicated by the fact that many sexual deviants, pulled in for questioning, made false confessions in a pitiful search for their fifteen minutes of fame.

A Brief Respite

Suddenly, in January, 1964, the murders stopped. The women of Boston cautiously began to breathe again. Could it be that the Strangler had moved elsewhere or – better still – had met with some fatal accident?

In hospital he confessed to the murders of 13 women

LEFT
J. B. Simons, Inc., the store on Western Avenue in Lynn, Mass., where DeSalvo was recaptured on 25 February, 1967, after being recognized by store employees. His fellow fugitives were recaptured on the previous night in Waltham, Mass.

Then, on 27 October, 1964, the Strangler struck again. Pretending to be a detective, he gained admission to the home of a young woman. He produced a knife and pinned her down on the bed. Then he bound her feet and hands and sexually assaulted her.

Inexplicably, the Strangler then rose from the bed and apologized to her before leaving the apartment. The girl struggled free of her bonds and called the police; she was able to give a full description of her assailant. The police identified him from

THE PSYCHOLOGY OF MASS-SLAYERS

In 1984 James Oliver Huberty massacred 21 people in a MacDonald's in San Ysidro, California. In 1988 former Marine sergeant, Gene Simmons, killed 16 people in Arkansas after being jilted by a girl. A few days later, copycat killer Robert Dreesman shot dead seven members of a family in a small town in Iowa.

Such explosive rampages are not confined to the United States. In August, 1991, a 33-year-old man went berserk with a rifle and a machete in a shopping plaza in Sydney, Australia. And in 1987, Michael Ryan killed 16 people as he stalked the streets of the English village of Hungerford, in Berkshire, with a Kalashnikov AK47 assault rifle.

George Hennard, with his record slaughter of 22 people in a restaurant in Texas, was, like all those rampage murderers, a loner. He was also a white, middle-class male. So far, no women have committed mass-murder.

The perpetrators are fairly well-off and live in affluent suburbs or the countryside. They are single or divorced and have no children. And they are not good with women. Often, they have a disturbed relationship with their mother. Whitman killed his wife and his mother before he climbed the tower. Michael Ryan's mother was his first victim.

George Hennard's mother was highly strung and domineering. He had often talked about killing her. After the carnage, she talked of a tragedy, the death of her beautiful son.

Mass-murderers almost always see themselves as failures. They cocoon themselves in a private world of television, cinema, videos and gun and survivalist magazines, which fuel their violent fantasies and promise relief – pouring indiscriminately from the barrel of a gun.

They begin to search for scapegoats. Some blame their teachers – there have been school-shootings even in relatively gun-free Great Britain. Others blame their bosses. One airline employee shot the pilot of a jet over California. Some blame women. Hennard may have been one of these.

Anything can spark the final murderous rampage – an outrageous phone bill, a snub from a girlfriend, a sidelong look in a restaurant. The killer then simply declares war on humanity.

RIGHT
Massachusetts State
Troopers seen with
rifles at the ready
during the search for
DeSalvo after his

escape. He got away
with George W.
Harrison, a convicted
armed robber, and
F. E. Erickson, a
convicted wife-slayer.

**RIGHT
Massachusetts State
Troopers seen with
rifles at the ready
during the search for
DeSalvo after his**

their records as Albert DeSalvo, who had
been released from prison in April, 1962,
following a conviction for indecent assault.

DeSalvo denied that he had been involved
with the murders, although he did confess
to housebreaking and rape. Psychiatrists
judged him to be schizophrenic and not
competent to stand trial. There was still no
firm evidence that he was the Boston
Strangler, but in hospital he confessed to
the murders of 13 women, describing both
the victims and the interiors of their homes.

The odd thing about the case was that
DeSalvo was never charged with being the
Boston Strangler. Instead, he was sentenced
to life imprisonment in 1967 for sex offences
and robberies committed before the murders. On 26 November, 1973, he was discovered in a pool of blood in his cell at
Walpole State Prison; he had been stabbed
through the heart.

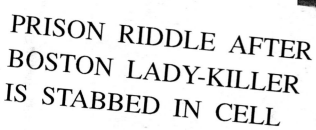

PRISON RIDDLE AFTER BOSTON LADY-KILLER IS STABBED IN CELL

LEFT
DeSalvo was
recaptured within 24
hours of his pre-dawn
prison break on 24
February, 1967. He is
seen here 35 minutes
after his capture in
Lynn, north of Boston.
He was disguised in
US Navy uniform.

RIGHT
An aerial view of the
correctional
institution at
Bridgewater,
Massachusetts, from
which the "Boston
Strangler" escaped
for a brief period in
February, 1967, soon
after being
committed.

"SON OF SAM": SCOURGE OF NEW YORK

Another infamous killer, the so-called "Son of Sam" subjected the city of New York to a 12-month reign of terror in 1976-77, during which time he killed seven people and wounded six others. Stalking the boroughs of Brooklyn, the Bronx and Queens, he preyed on courting couples in parked cars. His methods were always the same. On Saturday nights he simply walked up to the cars and opened fire on their occupants with a .44 Bulldog revolver. No more than four bullets were ever fired at his victims, but they were fired at point-blank range.

His first killing took place on 29 July, 1976, in the Bronx, when he approached a car, shot dead a young medical technician and wounded her companion. In October the scene of his crimes shifted to Queens, where he fired on and wounded another couple; in November – also in Queens – he calmly walked up to a couple in the street,

produced a revolver and opened fire. They fell to the ground, seriously wounded, but survived the attack. Police were in no doubt that the same man was involved, because bullets taken from the bodies of the victims matched the same weapon.

The attacks continued in the early months of 1977, when three more victims were shot to death. Two more were killed in the early

Plagued by rejection and tormented by voices

hours of 17 April, 1977, and this time detectives had a windfall. At the scene of the crime they found an envelope addressed to the New York Police Department. In it was a letter from the killer, berating the police

ABOVE
The so-called "Son of Sam" was an infamous serial killer who preyed on couples in parked cars. He subjected the city of New York to a 12-month reign of terror. Picture shows the 109th Precinct in Queens, NY.

for having described him as a woman-hater. His own description of himself was that he was a monster – the "Son of Sam".

Black Dogs and Demonic Voices

His last killing occurred on the night of 31 July, 1977. On this particular night, he made a serious mistake. He parked his car near a fire hydrant and was given a ticket. Police tracked him down to his home, where they found a loaded .44 Bulldog revolver on the seat of his car. They arrested him when he returned home.

The "Son of Sam" turned out to be a 24-year-old postal worker called David Berkowitz. A loner, he was plagued by feelings of rejection and said that he was constantly tormented by voices belonging to "demons" and by the barking of dogs, one

of which, a black labrador, was owned by a neighbour whose name was Sam.

Berkowitz pleaded guilty to the killings, asserting that the "voices" had been commanding him to kill since 1974. Psychiatrists who interviewed him were convinced that this story was false, designed to make them think that Berkowitz was insane. He was judged fit to stand trial, and in August, 1977, was sentenced to a total of 365 years' imprisonment. He admitted his guilt throughout the trial and made no attempt to appeal against the sentence.

THE KILLEEN KILLINGS

ABOVE
Police remove bodies from Luby's Cafeteria in Killeen, Texas, on the night of 16 October, 1991. Just hours earlier, a gunman had driven his truck through a plate-glass window and opened fire at the start of a 10-minute orgy of killing that left 23 people dead.

"Tell everybody Bell County was bad today"

At lunchtime on 16 October, 1991, 35-year-old George Hennard drove his truck through the plate-glass window of a crowded diner in Killeen, Texas, and began a 10-minute orgy of killing that left 23 people dead – the worst mass-shooting in America's history. "Texas, this is what you have done for me," Hennard shouted as he opened fire with two semi-automatic pistols.

The first victim was a man who had been hit by Hennard's truck. He was trying to get up when Hennard advanced on him. "Today is payday," said Hennard as he shot him. A child cried: "He's just shot daddy."

Then Hennard turned on the lunch queue and started picking off the customers one by one. In his blue T-shirt and dark glasses, he had the blank look of the robot from *The Terminator*. When his guns were empty, he coolly changed the magazines and continued the slaughter. More than 100 spent cartridges were found in the wreckage.

WOMAN-HATER

The killings may have been motivated by a pathological hatred of women. In a letter to his sisters, Jill Fritz and Jana Jernignan, he referred to "the abundance of evil women"

ABOVE
This 1987 photograph of the killer, George Hennard of Belton, Texas, is from a Department of Public Safety file. Later, it was thought that the massacre in Killeen may have been motivated by a pathological hatred of women.

and "female viper" in Killeen and his home town of Belton. Of his 22 victims, 14 were women. Hennard shouted "You bitch" at one woman before pumping bullets into her defenceless body. Yet he told another woman, Anica McNeil, with her four-year-old daughter Lakeshia, to "get your baby and get out of here". "Tell everybody Bell County was bad today," he said. Anica's mother, Olga Taylor, who was lunching with her daughter and grand-daughter, was coldly gunned down by the killer.

Distraught women hid under the tables, screaming and crying. Another, hiding in the toilets with her daughter, dodged bullets ricocheting off the walls. Tommy Vaughan, a 23-stone car mechanic, smashed through the back window and 15 people managed to scramble to safety as the gunman bore down on them. The rest were murdered with the calmness of a professional executioner.

"WORSE THAN VIETNAM"

After 10 minutes the wailing of police sirens was heard. In the ensuing gun battle, Hennard was hit twice. He staggered to the back of the restaurant, where, without hesitation, he turned his gun on himself.

Rescuers found a scene of appalling horror. Bodies lay scattered among a battlefield of upturned tables. The wounded were helicoptered to an army hospital in the vicinity – Fort Hood.

"It was worse than anything I saw in Vietnam," said one medic.

Twelve hours later, one of the restaurant's employees, Mark Mathews, was found alive, hiding in a dishwasher.

ABOVE
Officials investigate the scene of the shooting at Luby's Cafeteria, Killeen. Hennard opened fire with two semi-automatic pistols; when the guns were empty he coolly changed the magazines and went on shooting at the hysterical diners.

RIGHT
Workers pick up flowers left at the scene of the massacre. Hennard was hit twice in a gun battle with police and staggered into the back of the restaurant, where he shot himself. One terrified employee was found hiding in a dishwasher twelve hours later.

FAME, FORTUNE AND RANSOM

To be super-rich is to be vulnerable to abduction by kidnappers. Three millionaire American families - the Lindberghs, the Hearsts and the Gettys - learned the lesson to their cost and their heartache. And sometimes there is a twist to the tale - how to tell the kidnapped from the kidnapper?

CHARLES LINDBERGH: THE HARROWING OF AN AMERICAN HERO

Charles Lindbergh, the first man to fly solo across the Atlantic, was an all-American hero. The kidnapping and subsequent murder of his 20-month-old son shocked the world.

Lindbergh was just 25 when he flew the Atlantic in *The Spirit of St Louis* in 1927. Five years later, he was a rich and famous man. He had married the daughter of the banker and diplomat, Dwight Morrow, one of the richest men in America. A year later, in 1930, Charles Lindbergh Jr was born.

An Empty Crib

On the evening of Tuesday, 1 March, 1932, with the baby in bed, Charles and Anne Lindbergh were chatting in their country house at Hopewell, New Jersey. Soon after 9 pm, Lindbergh heard a noise that sounded like wood cracking. But his wife said she heard nothing.

Shortly after 10 pm, Charles Jr's nurse went to check on the baby. She found the crib empty. Betty Gow checked to see whether Mrs Lindbergh had the baby. She did not. It soon transpired that Mr Lindbergh did not have him either.

Lindbergh ran upstairs to the nursery. There was mud on a chest near the window. On the window sill lay an envelope. Lindbergh ordered that nothing be touched until the room had been checked for fingerprints. He called the police. When the police arrived they found a home-made ladder outside the baby's window. Nearby lay a chisel.

After the police had fingerprinted the nursery, finding nothing, Lindbergh opened the envelope. Inside was a badly spelt note: "Dear Sir! Have 50 000 $ redy 25 000 $ in

ABOVE
Charles Lindbergh pictured after his solo flight across the North Atlantic in 1927. His exploit made him a hero in the eyes of the world; many aviators had attempted the feat before him, only to vanish without trace.

ABOVE
Lindbergh's Ryan monoplane, the *Spirit of St Louis*. To make possible the long-distance transatlantic flight, the aircraft was virtually transformed into a flying fuel tank.

20 $ bills 15 000 $ in 10 $ bills and 10 000 $ in 5 $ bills. After 2–4 days we will inform you were to deliver the mony. We warn you for making anyding public or for notify the police. The child is in gut care. Indication for all letters are signature and 3 holds." At the bottom there were two circles in blue. Where they overlapped was a third circle in red ink.

Newspapers blared the story to the world. The jailed gangster, Al Capone, offered his help to find the baby – in exchange for his freedom. A wealthy socialite, Evelyn Walsh McLean, offered to pay twice the $50,000 ransom for the return of the Lindbergh baby – and was quickly relieved of $100,000 by two con men. Another upper-class adventurer, John Hughes Curtis, held daily press conferences in which he talked about his contact with the kidnappers. The police discovered that his stories were fabricated.

"Cemetery John"

The kidnappers did get in touch with Dr John Francis Condon, a columnist for the Bronx *Home News*. He arranged a meeting in a cemetery, where a shadowy figure asked, in a German accent, if he "would burn if the baby was dead". He insisted that the baby was well, but he was plainly afraid of the electric chair.

BELOW RIGHT
New Jersey State police begin an inch-by-inch search of the grounds of Charles Lindbergh's estate at Hopewell, New Jersey, in the hope of finding a vital clue to the child's disappearance. What followed was to develop into the biggest manhunt in American history.

LEFT
Charles Lindbergh Jr. The child was kidnapped on the evening of 1 March, 1932, while Charles and his wife Anne were chatting at home. It was the baby's nurse who found the crib empty when she went to check shortly after 10 pm.

LEFT
Arthur Koehler, of the Forest products laboratory, Madison, Wisconsin, examines the ladder used in the Lindbergh kidnapping. His task was to find marks that correspond with tools found in the possession of Bruno R. Hauptmann, who was indicted with the crime.

Another meeting was arranged with the man, who quickly became known as "Cemetery John". Condon, on Lindbergh's behalf, handed over the ransom money, much of it in old-fashioned gold certificates that were easy to trace. A note given to Condon said the baby would be found on a boat named *Nelly* near the Elizabeth Islands off the coast of Massachusetts.

Lindbergh looked for days, but the boat was never found. Then, 10 weeks after the kidnapping, a truck driver stumbled across the body of Charles Jr, his foot jutting from a shallow grave in a wood just four and a

Charles Jr.'s foot was jutting from a shallow grave

half miles from the Lindberghs' Hopewell mansion. He had been killed shortly after the kidnapping.

With few clues to go on, the police turned their attention to the Lindberghs' servants. The constant interrogations drove the 28-year-old English-born maid, Betty Gow, to suicide. The German-born gardener took his own life a short time later.

Bills from the ransom payment began to turn up, but the police could never track them to their source. Then, in 1933, the US

RIGHT
Comparison between Hauptmann's handwriting and that on the ransom notes. The two matched, forming key evidence when the abductor came to be prosecuted.

Treasury called in all their remaining gold certificates in circulation, making it harder for "Cemetery John" to pass his certificates without being detected.

A Man Who Could Make Ladders

More than two years after the kidnapping, on 16 September, 1934, a New York gas station took a $10 gold certificate. The owner wrote down the licence-plate number of the driver's car and the car was traced to Bruno Richard Hauptmann, a German immigrant. He was an unemployed carpenter – a man who could make ladders.

Hauptmann lived in the Bronx, where the newspaper that carried Dr Condon's column was distributed. In a secret panel behind his workbench, the police found a gun, maps and gold certificates. The serial numbers matched those of the ransom certificates. Hauptmann said that the money had been left by a fellow immigrant, Isidore Fisch, who had returned to Germany and died there. Hauptmann's handwriting also matched the ransom notes.

In court, Lindbergh said that he recognized Hauptmann's voice as Cemetery John's, a voice he had heard only once, two and a half years earlier. A nearly blind, 87-year-old witness also placed Hauptmann near Hopewell on the night of the kidnapping.

Hauptmann claimed that he was working that night. His supervisor corroborated his story, but the time-sheets could not be found. Hauptmann did not know the Hopewell area and could not have known that the baby was there that night. But the prosecution made a meal of him. Hauptmann, they said, was a proto-Nazi, the sort of man who could kill an innocent child, then coolly demand a ransom payment. They even claimed that, in the blue-and-red "three hole" signature, Bruno Richard Hauptmann had spelt out his initials – blue for the B, red for the R and the holes for the H.

Hauptmann was found guilty of kidnapping and murder. But as his execution approached, many people, including President Roosevelt's wife, Eleanor, expressed their disquiet. While Hauptmann waited on death row, gold bills from the ransom continued to be passed and a key prosecution witness was arrested for theft.

Bruno Richard Hauptmann went to the electric chair at Trenton State Prison, New Jersey, on 3 April, 1936, still refusing to admit his guilt.

SOME LESSER-KNOWN ABDUCTIONS . . .

In 1532 the rapacious Spanish *conquistador*, Francisco Pizarro, pulled off history's biggest kidnapping stunt. He captured the Inca king, Atahualpa, and demanded a hall filled with gold and silver in exchange for the captive's release. In modern money, the amount would have been worth $170 million.

That total has never been surpassed, but some staggering sums of money have been handed over. In June, 1975, for example, 1,500 million pesos – $60 million – was paid to a left-wing urban guerrilla group called the Montoneros in Buenos Aires, to secure the release of the businessmen, Jorge and Juan Born.

Extorting money is the traditional motive for kidnapping, but in recent years the crime has been increasingly associated with the sexual abuse and murder of the victim.

In the late 1970s, several young women went missing in the vicinity of Anchorage, Alaska. Some were prostitutes, others night-club dancers.

The first body, that of the topless dancer Sherry Morrow, was found by two hunters in a shallow grave on the banks of the Knik River in September, 1982. Shell casings in the grave indicated that she had been shot by a high-velocity, .223 calibre Ruger Mini-14 rifle, an unusual weapon used by hunters for long-range work.

Police eventually tracked down the killer, a 44-year-old bakery proprietor named Robert Hanson. Outwardly respectable, a well-known big-game hunter, he was the last person anyone would suspect of kidnapping and assaulting women. His strategy was to handcuff them and take them to a remote spot outside Anchorage in his car or private plane. Then he would let them go and hunt them as they ran terrified and stark naked through the woods, almost always killing them at long range.

In his confession, Hanson stated that he had raped more than 30 women and killed at least 20. In February, 1984, he was sentenced to a total of 461 years' imprisonment on various counts of kidnapping, rape and murder.

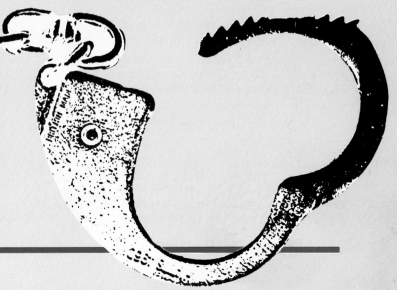

PATTY HEARST: "URBAN GUERRILLA"

The American media heiress, Patty Hearst, was a celebrated kidnap victim who joined the gang. From being an innocent 19-year-old abducted by a self-styled liberation army, she quickly turned into a hard-faced, gun-toting terrorist – just to stay alive.

On the evening of 4 February, 1974, two men dragged Patty Hearst, half-naked, from the apartment of her boyfriend, Steven Weed, in Berkeley, California. Struggling and screaming, she was driven off in the boot of an old Chevrolet. The kidnappers left a box of cyanide-tipped bullets in Weed's apartment. The police recognized the calling card of the SLA – the Symbionese Liberation Army – an urban terrorist group who had declared war on the "fascist state of Amerikkka". The three Ks referred to the Ku Klux Klan.

Three days after the kidnapping, a communiqué from the SLA, sent to a local radio station, announced that Patty Hearst was a prisoner of war. The communiqué closed with the slogan: "Death to the fascist insect that preys on the life of the people".

A few days later the radio station received a cassette. Patty's voice was on it. She told her parents that she was blindfolded, but otherwise was being treated well. Then a man, who identified himself as General Field-Marshall Cinque, demanded that the "Hearst Fascist-Corporation Empire" give $70-worth of top-quality food to everyone in California who held a welfare card.

Patty's father, Randolph Hearst, was shocked to discover that there were almost six million people on welfare in America's richest state. Paying the ransom would cost

RIGHT
Heiress Patty Hearst pictured on vacation in Corfu before being abducted. She quickly changed from an innocent 19-year-old into a hard-bitten urban guerrilla, possibly in order to save her own life.

the Hearst Corporation a crippling amount of money – $415 million.

Patty had fallen into the hands of a small-time crook, a black named Donald DeFreeze. A native of Detroit, he had taken to crime at the age of 14 and had frequently been arrested for possessing firearms and bombs.

War on the "fascist state of Amerikkka"

During the 1965 Watts riots, DeFreeze became a police informer. In return, the police overlooked eight offences ranging from burglary to kidnapping. But in 1971, after DeFreeze had stolen $1,000 from a woman at gunpoint, he was sent to the psychiatric facility at Vacaville prison. There he was introduced to revolutionary politics by two prison visitors.

Shortly after he was transferred to Soledad prison in 1973, he escaped and made his way to Berkeley's famous "Peking House" – a centre for revolutionary intellectuals and

ABOVE LEFT
Patty's grandfather, William Randolph Hearst, seen here on the left, was an influential newspaper baron. Her parents said that she had shown signs of a "rebellious nature" at school.

LEFT
This picture, released by the FBI on 15 April, 1974, was taken by a surveillance camera of the Hibernia Bank in San Francisco. A bank robbery is taking place. The FBI said that the girl in the photograph, who is armed, resembled Patty Hearst, but said that she might have been acting under duress; other photos showed that someone else was holding a gun on her.

the home of his prison visitors, Nancy Ling Perry and Patricia Soltysik. DeFreeze took the name "Cinque" after a rebellious slave and moved his weird ragbag of middle-class white followers to Oakland.

Their first "revolutionary" act was the murder of a black school superintendent, Marcus Foster. He was shot with cyanide-tipped bullets because he endorsed a "fascist" plan to photograph all Oakland students for identification purposes. The two assassins, Russell Little and Joseph Remiro, were captured after a gun-battle, and some nights later, after a blaze at the SLA's bomb factory, the police found a notebook with an entry saying: "Patricia Campbell Hearst on the night of the full moon of January 7". They took no notice.

Unable to meet the ransom demand in full, Randolph Hearst started People In

When asked her occupation, she replied staunchly: "Urban guerrilla"

Need, which distributed food parcels worth $2 million to the poor. DeFreeze was not satisfied. To a man of Hearst's wealth, he raged, $2 million was a drop in the ocean. Patty agreed, on a tape the kidnappers sent.

"Patria o Muerte"

Patty had begun to realize the dangerous position she was in. The media were criticizing her for her "rebellion", especially her use of marijuana and openly living with a man whom she did not intend to marry. The FBI, Patty felt, was itching to gun down the SLA – and would not be too worried if she were caught in the crossfire.

She decided that the way to survive was to join her captors. She cut her hair, took the revolutionary nickname, "Tania" (after the revolutionary who had fought alongside Che Guevara in Bolivia), and became the lover of DeFreeze and another SLA member, Willie Wolfe. Her new tapes spouted the revolutionary slogan: "Patria o muerte, Venceremos!" ("Homeland or death, we shall overcome").

The Hearst family refused to recognize this change of heart. But the world at large was convinced when Patty joined DeFreeze in a raid on the Hibernia Bank in San Francisco's Sunset District on 15 April, 1974. Video footage of Patty menacing the bank's customers, taken by security cameras, was shown on television and Attorney General William B Saxbe publicly labelled her a common criminal.

A month later two members of the gang – Bill and Emily Harris – were caught shoplifting in Mel's Sporting Goods store in Los Angeles. Patty opened fire with an automatic from a van outside and under the covering fire the Harrises made their escape.

An SLA informer told the police that the gang was holed up in a small stucco house at 1466 East 54th Street, Los Angeles. A 375-strong task force, including a heavily armed SWAT team, surrounded the building. They fired a CS gas canister into the house and a full-scale gun-battle ensued.

Forty minutes later black smoke began to billow from the back of the house and flames were seen through the window. The police gave the gang a final chance to give up. Nobody emerged.

But at the last moment, while their comrades burned to death in the crawl-space beneath the floor, Camilla Hall and Nancy Ling Perry made a break for it. Hall's head got stuck in a ventilation duct. The police killed her with a single shot through the forehead. Perry managed to crawl halfway across the garden before her body was riddled with more than 20 bullets.

ABOVE
Patty Hearst testifying in San Francisco at a special hearing convened in January, 1976, to investigate complaints about the conduct of one of the psychiatrists who had examined her in jail. She claimed that his questions had driven her to hysteria. The courtroom sketch is by artist Walt Stewart.

On the Run

Two days later, it was confirmed that Patty Hearst and the Harrises were not among the charred bodies in the house. Now on the run, they went on a spree of bank robberies, car thefts, abductions and bombings. Patty seemed almost relieved when the FBI agent, Tom Padden, burst into her apartment on 18 September, 1975 – 20 months after her abduction. At the precinct, when she was asked her occupation, she replied staunchly: "Urban guerrilla".

Although Patty recanted her revolutionary credo and claimed to have been a "prisoner of war" throughout, she was found guilty of bank robbery and was sentenced to seven years in a federal penitentiary.

After she had served 23 months, the FBI chief who had led the hunt for her wrote to the Attorney General asking for clemency. And on 29 January, 1979, President Carter personally commuted her sentence.

LEFT
Patty Hearst is escorted by Deputy US Marshal Janey Jimenez as they leave for the San Mateo County Jail in March, 1976, after a court appearance at the San Francisco Federal Building. When asked her occupation, Hearst replied: "Urban gueriila".

KIDNAPPING – AN AMERICAN CRIME?

Kidnapping is a characteristically American crime. In the early years of this century there were 10 premeditated abductions a year in the United States – and hostage-taking during robberies was commonplace.

The Lindbergh case only fanned the flames. In the three years after the murder of Charles Lindbergh Jr, there were 48 recorded cases of kidnapping. Even though in certain states – like Illinois, home of the Chicago mobsters – kidnapping attracted the death-sentence, many small-time hoodlums on the make considered it worth the risk. The sheer size of the country made it possible to disappear easily; kidnapping was a crime that offered a good chance of success.

In smaller European countries kidnapping was more risky and, consequently, rarer. In the late 1960s, for example, when Muriel McKay was abducted, Scotland Yard had to turn to the American police for advice. It was the first kidnapping in Great Britain for nearly 800 years.

The Lindbergh case raised such a political furore that in June, 1933, kidnapping became a federal offence. Under the so-called Lindbergh law, the FBI was placed in charge of any kidnapping case. Previously they had had to wait seven days to give the kidnappers a fair chance to transport their victim across a state line, thereby making it a Federal offence.

It is not uncommon for kidnap victims like Patty Hearst to feel close to, and even take the side of, their abductors. This is known as the Stockholm syndrome, after a failed bank-raid in the Swedish capital in 1974. Police surrounded the building before the gunmen could make their getaway and the robbers held customers hostage in the bank for five days before finally giving up. By that time, the bond between the gunmen and their hostages had become strong. Later, a female victim married one of her captors.

THE ILL-FORTUNE OF JEAN-PAUL GETTY III

Jean-Paul Getty III was the grandson of the richest man in the world, the US oil billionaire, J. Paul Getty. In Rome, where the wayward 17-year-old lived in 1973, he was known as "The Golden Hippy". He slept all day and spent his nights in discos. His name opened doors for him and attracted girls. He loved to drive fast and he earned a little money posing nude for magazines. With his actress girlfriend, he hung out with Andy Warhol, Jack Nicholson, Faye Dunaway, Roman Polanski, Mick Jagger and the Rolling Stones. Despite his family's wealth, he had to live on a small allowance, and he once remarked that the only way he could finance his lifestyle was to fake his own kidnapping.

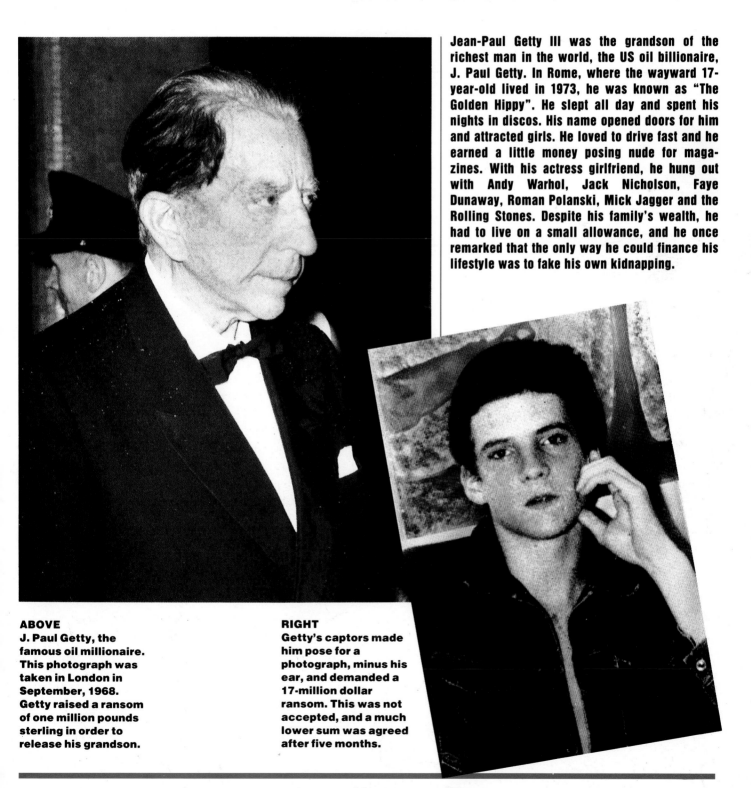

ABOVE
J. Paul Getty, the famous oil millionaire. This photograph was taken in London in September, 1968. Getty raised a ransom of one million pounds sterling in order to release his grandson.

RIGHT
Getty's captors made him pose for a photograph, minus his ear, and demanded a 17-million dollar ransom. This was not accepted, and a much lower sum was agreed after five months.

A Kidnap Not Believed

In the early hours of 10 July, 1973, Jean-Paul Getty III staggered drunkenly from a nightclub in the Via de Mascarone in Rome. A large white car pulled up in front of him. Three armed men grabbed him from behind. They beat him over the head with pistol butts and bundled him into the car. Getty did not take the kidnapping seriously. He thought he had been arrested by the police.

His mother, the former actress Gail Harris, thought he had run off with a girl and refused to cooperate with the Italian police. And when the kidnappers demanded $17 million for his return, the boy's grandfather responded that he did not pay extortion. "If I pay one penny now, I'll have 14 kidnapped grandchildren."

CHAINED UP FOR MONTHS ON END

Getty had been abducted by the Calabrian mafia and taken to the barren region at the toe of Italy's boot – 250 miles from Rome. He was kept blindfolded and moved from place to place. When his blindfold was removed, he would find his captors masked. If one of their masks slipped, he was told, he would be killed. The kidnappers were armed with Berettas, rifles, machine-guns and sawn-off shotguns. They smoked Marlboro cigarettes incessantly and acted like American gangsters.

Getty was chained up in rough shacks or caves, for months. Sometimes he was not allowed to go to the toilet alone. Someone would have to take down his pants. His food was poor and he was forced to walk for miles in mountainous country, blindfolded.

An Ear for Proof

After three months in which no notice was taken of their ransom demand, the kidnappers decided on a new tack.

One day they cut Getty's hair and disinfected his head. Getty then waited an hour while his captors sharpened a razor. They fed him, and when he had finished eating, put a handkerchief in his mouth, held his arms behind his back and put his head down on a chopping block. With one swift stroke they slashed his ear off.

Getty bled for three days and the overriding thought that passed through his mind was that he would never be able to wear sunglasses again.

His captors made him pose for a photograph, which they sent, along with the ear, in an envelope to the Rome newspaper, *Il Messaggero*.

A postal strike was just then crippling southern Italy and it took nearly three weeks before the Polaroid, the ear and a few blood-soaked strands of hair turned up at the newspaper's office.

A THIRD CAR PULLED OFF THE ROAD

The paper called Gail Harris. When she turned up at the newspaper's office, she picked up the ear, felt it, noted it was freckled and identified it as her son's. J. Paul Getty Snr sent a business associate, Fletcher Chase, a former CIA-man, to Italy with 2 billion lire (around $2 million) in small bills.

Following the kidnappers' instructions, Chase drove a rented car south from Naples. Outside the village of Lagonegro, a Citroën

pulled alongside. The window was wound down and pebbles thrown at Chase's car. This was the sign to pull over. While the ransom money was being paid, a third car pulled off the road. In it were a man and a woman pretending to be tourists. They were to identify the kidnappers.

The Victim Under Suspicion

Some time later, Jean-Paul Getty was dropped off on an autostrada, five months after he was kidnapped. He started hitch-hiking. No one stopped. He lay down, pretending to be dead. Drivers took no notice. He walked to the nearest petrol station. It had no phone. Eventually, a truck stopped and Getty told the driver who he was. The

ABOVE
Jean-Paul Getty III, grandson of the oil magnate, pictured with his bride, a West German actress, after their marriage in Italy. The wedding took place in the year after Getty was kidnapped and released following payment of a huge ransom.

driver, thinking he was crazy, drove off and made for the police station in the next town. The town was Lagonegro.

Jean-Paul Getty was just being refused another lift when the police turned up – and arrested him. The *carabinieri* – the police militia – did not believe that Getty had been kidnapped. Believing that he was behind an elaborate plan to defraud his grandfather, they subjected him to interrogation. Chase had to threaten them with a major scandal before they would release him.

Chase and his "tourists" identified eight members of the Calabrian mafia, and two of them, Antonio Marcuso and Giuseppe Lamanna – the latter identified as the razor-wielding assailant – went to jail for eight and 16 years respectively.

CRIMES OF PASSION PERVERTED

Sexuality perverted into hatred and cruelty has produced some of the most chilling murders of the century. And when such crimes are the work of serial killers, they touch depths of almost unspeakable anguish and horror.

JEFFREY DAHMER: "THE MILWAUKEE CANNIBAL"

In July, 1991, police in the American city of Milwaukee made what ranks as one of the most gruesome discoveries in the history of crime. In a stinking, fly-infested flat they found the remains of at least 11 men, all of them black. They had been dismembered.

Amid conditions which the police spokesman, Phillip Arreola, said were "indescribable", police found four intact bodies, parts of seven others and 11 skulls. There were also five whole skeletons, a kettle containing human hands and a vat of acid believed to have been used to dissolve human remains.

One of the first policemen to enter the apartment opened the refrigerator to find the preserved heads of three men. Another found a drawer stuffed full of photographs showing dismembered bodies and men involved in homosexual acts.

The apartment was the home of Jeffrey

RIGHT
One of the young men in this photograph, 33-year-old Ricky Becks of Milwaukee, was positively identified as one of the victims found in Dahmer's apartment. All the young men slain by Dahmer are said to have been black.

BELOW
Jeffrey Dahmer, the "meek guy" who killed and dismembered 17 young men in Milwaukee in 1991 and allegedly ate parts of their bodies. The killer, aged 31, worked in a chocolate factory.

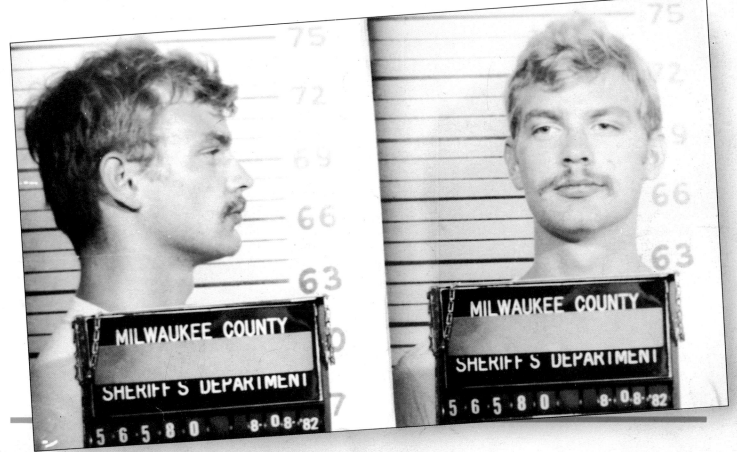

LEFT
Two men wearing protective chemical suits and breathing apparatus remove a barrel containing dismembered body parts from Dahmer's apartment. It was the stench from the apartment that first alerted neighbours to Dahmer's fearful activities.

BELOW
Jeffrey Dahmer makes his initial appearance at the Milwaukee Circuit Court, where he is charged with four counts of first-degree intentional homicide. One intended victim, despite being handcuffed, escaped a frenzied attack with a butcher's knife.

fact that the saws were being used for a more sinister purpose emerged when a man in handcuffs escaped from the apartment and told police that Dahmer had tried to attack him with a butcher's knife.

In police custody, the man described by neighbours as "such a meek guy" admitted killing 17 young men in a rampage of necrophilia, dismemberment and possible cannibalism. He pleaded insanity.

Dahmer, a 31-year-old chocolate-factory worker. In 1989 he was convicted of sexual assault for offering money to a 13-year-old boy to pose nude; he was released on probation. Earlier, in 1986, he had been convicted for indecent exposure.

Neighbours had complained about a stench from Dahmer's flat on and off for about a year. Others reported hearing power-saws buzzing at odd hours; they had assumed that Dahmer was building something. The

ABOVE LEFT
Milwaukee police officers look over evidence gathered at Dahmer's apartment. Detectives found body parts stored in a freezer as well as in barrels. Clothing belonging to the victims was packed away in cardboard boxes.

THE "YORKSHIRE RIPPER"

The man they called Jack the Ripper, the still-unidentified killer who stalked the sleazy streets of London's Whitechapel district in the 1880s and left a trail of murdered, mutilated prostitutes in his wake, is a criminal legend. Nearly a century later, in a string of carbon-copy murders that left police baffled, a similar nightmare descended upon the county of Yorkshire, England. In a five-year period, beginning in 1975, 20 women – most, but not all, prostitutes – were attacked. Thirteen died brutally; seven survived, often with horrific injuries. The tools of the so-called Yorkshire Ripper's trade were the hammer and the knife.

War on Prostitutes

The terror started in the early hours of 5 July, 1975, in a cobbled street in the town of Keighley. Anna Rogulskyj returned home after a drinking session in a Bradford night club to find that her boyfriend had apparently walked out on her and went to the house where he normally lived. She pounded

on the door for a while, then smashed a ground-floor window with one of her high-heeled shoes.

As she stooped to replace the shoe on her foot, a figure emerged from the shadows and smashed her skull in three places with a

A figure emerged from the shadows

hammer. As she lay unconscious, her assailant raised her skirt and slashed her stomach in a frenzied attack before melting away into the night.

Anna was discovered at 2.20 am and was rushed to Leeds General Infirmary, critically ill. She survived, but was unable to give

ABOVE
Peter William Sutcliffe, the man eventually identified as the "Yorkshire Ripper". Thirteen of his victims died brutally but seven survived, albeit often with terrible injuries. His reign of terror began in the early hours of 5 July, 1975.

ABOVE
While the hunt for the Ripper was at its height, some bloodstained clothing was found by the side of the Darlington-Staindrop road in
County Durham. It was a false lead, although it was later established that the Ripper had in fact stayed in Darlington at a guest house for a short time.

police any worthwhile information about the attack, or the attacker.

Five weeks later a housewife, Olive Smelt, returning home after a night out with friends in Halifax, was also violently attacked. She, too, survived, but had no memory of the assault at all.

Wilma McCann was not so lucky. At 7.41 am on 30 October, 1975, a milkman stumbled upon her mutilated, partially-clad body in the Prince Philip Playing Fields, Leeds City. The 26-year-old prostitute and mother of four young children had suffered multiple stab wounds to the abdomen, chest and throat, and her skull had been brutally crushed by a hammer.

A murder hunt involving 150 police officers of Leeds CID, led by Chief Superintendent Dennis Hoban, was immediately launched. Weeks passed, and the investigation got nowhere. But Hoban, a veteran criminal investigator, was convinced that the killer would strike again. He was right.

On 20 November, 1975, another prostitute, Joan Harrison, was murdered in Preston,

Lancashire. She had been beaten to death with a hammer. Forensic tests established that she had had sexual intercourse shortly before her death, perhaps with her assailant. There was distinctive bite mark on her breast. Yet Lancashire CID did not link her death with Wilma McCann's; it was thought that a local man was responsible, or possibly a sailor from one of the ships at anchor in Preston's harbour.

ABOVE
Police officers at the spot where the body of Barbara Leach was found on 2 September, 1979. Barbara, a 20-year-old student, was murdered by the Ripper within seven minutes of leaving the Bradford public house where she had been drinking with friends.

ABOVE LEFT
Police officers examine the body of Vera Millward, found on wasteland in Livingstone Street, Manchester, on 17 May, 1978. Millward, 41, was a prostitute; she had been killed by blows to the head and had also suffered stab wounds.

On 21 December, 1975, a Leeds house-wife, Emily Jackson, tormented by mounting debts, turned to prostitution as a means of paying the bills. Every evening she would drive to the Gaiety public house, and while her husband sat at the bar she sought clients in the neighbouring streets. On 20 January, 1976, she met her last customer. The following morning the body of the 42-year-old was found in a derelict building. She had suffered severe injuries to the skull and had been stabbed at least 50 times.

On 6 February, 1977, the body of yet another victim was found at Soldiers Field, Leeds. Twenty-eight years old, the mother of two children, she was unemployed and

While her husband sat at the bar she sought clients

virtually homeless. She had been beaten to death and had suffered horrific mutilation. Her name was Irene Richardson.

Richardson's boyfriend, an absconder from prison named Steven Bray, was tracked down and arrested. But after intensive questioning, Bray was eliminated from the inquiry and returned to prison.

On 23 April, 1977, the Ripper struck again. The battered body of a prostitute named Tina Atkinson was discovered in a block of flats in Bradford. Even as the police were compiling a dossier on this new crime, a 16-year-old Leeds shop assistant, Jayne MacDonald, met her death in the same brutal manner. Last seen alive in a beer celler on the evening of 25 June, 1977, she was found in an adventure playground on the following morning.

On 9 July, 1977, the Ripper once again prowled the streets of Bradford. He offered a lift to a woman called Maureen Long. She was found the next morning on waste ground with a fractured skull and stab wounds to her abdomen and back. She should have been dead, but was not, and managed to give a description of the attacker to the police.

The officer who interviewed her as she lay seriously ill in hospital was Assistant Chief Constable George Oldfield, a man with more than 30 years' police experience, who had been put in charge of the investigation into the Ripper killings. For Oldfield the hunt for the Ripper had become an intensely personal affair.

The victims

1. WILMA McCANN, 28 LEEDS, OCTOBER 1975
2. EMILY JACKSON, 42 LEEDS, JANUARY 1976
3. IRENE RICHARDSON, 28 LEEDS, FEBRUARY 1977
4. PATRICIA ATKINSON, 32 BRADFORD, APRIL 1977
5. JAYNE McDONALD, 16 LEEDS, JUNE 1977
6. JEAN JORDAN, 21 MANCHESTER, OCTOBER 1977
7. YVONNE PEARSON, 22 BRADFORD, JANUARY 1978
8. HELEN RYTKA, 18 HUDDERSFIELD, JANUARY 1978
9. VERA MILLWARD, 41 MANCHESTER, MAY 1978
10. JOSEPHINE WHITAKER, 19 HALIFAX, APRIL 1979
11. BARBARA LEACH, 20 BRADFORD, SEPTEMBER 1979
12. JACQUELINE HILL, 20 LEEDS, NOVEMBER 1980

On 1 October, 1977, Jean Jordan, also known as Jean Royle – Alan Royle was the man she lived with – left her flat in Hulme, Manchester, "for a breath of fresh air". She never returned. The Ripper picked her up, smashed her skull, and hid her body on waste land.

A week later, he returned to the scene of the crime and mutilated the corpse. It was found by a workman the next day. And on 15 October the murdered prostitute's handbag was also found, lying less than 100 yards from her body. It had been rifled, but in a side pocket was a crisp, new five-pound note.

A Bungled Lead

The note had gone into circulation in the Bradford area four days before Jean Jordan was murdered, and would not have ended up in somebody's pay packet until Thursday or Friday, the day of her death. The police knew that it could not have come into her possession as the result of a normal commercial transaction in the time available; it must have been given to her by the killer.

ABOVE
Twelve victims of the Yorkshire Ripper who were killed between October 1975 and November 1980. Jacqueline Hill (bottom right), a student at Leeds University, was the last.

The fact that Jean Jordan's handbag lay undiscovered so close to her body for five days did the police no credit. And they failed to release the information about the bank note, with its serial number, for a further 12 days. By that time it was too late. Although the police identified the firms to which five-

He returned to mutilate the corpse

pound notes in that particular batch had been issued, the money had been scattered far and wide, changing hands many times.

Detectives from Greater Manchester and West Yorkshire joined forces to interview all the employees of the firms involved. They even, without knowing it, interviewed the killer. If the handbag had been found sooner, and if the police had taken rapid action on the bank note, seven women would probably still be alive and another three would have escaped serious attacks.

But on the night of 14 December, 1977, an attractive prostitute named Marilyn Moore, 25 years old, was picked up in Chapeltown, the red-light district of Leeds, by a man in a Ford Corsair. He drove to some waste ground, but when he refused to pay in advance Moore argued with him and got out. He followed her and smashed her several times on the head with a hammer, then – thinking he saw a light go on in a caravan some distance away – drove off without using the knife on her.

Marilyn Moore was found by a passer-by an hour later. She had managed to stagger as far as a telephone box. She was able to describe her attacker and the interior of his car. It was another description to add to the growing pile. There were many descriptions, but no two of them agreed.

On 21 January, 1978, a Bradford call-girl, Yvonne Pearson, walked out of the city's Flying Dutchman pub to solicit a client. She simply vanished. Ten days later, police in Huddersfield were notified that another prostitute had gone missing; she was 18-year-old Helen Rytka, a Jamaican woman. In the afternoon of 3 February, her naked, mutilated body was discovered partially hidden in a woodyard.

The "Ripper Letters"
On 10 March, 1978, Assistant Chief Constable George Oldfield received the first of the "Ripper Letters" that were to divert a vast amount of effort into what turned out

to be a wild goose chase. The letter had been posted in Sunderland, and the writer confessed to being the Ripper. Certain details in it – a reference to the murder in Preston in 1975, for instance – led Oldfield to believe

The "Ripper Letters" turned out to be a wild goose chase

that it was real. A few days later a letter in the same hand was sent to the *Daily Mirror*.

On 26 March, while this lead was being investigated, the body of Yvonne Pearson was found on waste ground in Bradford. Death was due to massive head injuries, caused by something like a heavy rock. On the face of it, there seemed to be no connection between this killing and the Ripper murders. It did not fit the pattern.

The next one did. On 17 May, 1978, the body of Vera Millward was found on waste

ABOVE
Bradford lorry driver Peter Sutcliffe, shielded from cameras by a blanket, shown after his arrest. At Leeds Crown Court, he was charged with the murder of 13 women and the attempted murder of seven more. He was sentenced to life imprisonment, with a recommendation that he should serve no less than 30 years.

land in Livingstone Street, Manchester. A convicted prostitute, she was 41 years old but looked 15 years older. She had been killed by blows to the head and had suffered stab wounds in the abdomen and back.

The Ripper investigation was now in the hands of a specially-formed Prostitute Murder Squad, a team of 12 hand-picked men led by Detective Chief Superintendent John Domaille of Bradford CID. Domaille's first task was to win over the prostitutes. It was a hard task, but the prostitutes' fear of the Ripper was greater than their fear of the police. They agreed to work only in certain designated areas where detectives could keep an eye on them.

The new tactics did not prevent the murder of 19-year-old Josephine Whitaker, slaughtered on the night of 4 April, 1979, and found in Saville Park, Halifax.

George Oldfield, who had been coordinating the manhunt from behind his desk while Domaille's team worked out in the field, once again found himself working a 16-hour day. Domaille, badly in need of a rest, was promoted to the position of Commander of the Police Academy at Wakefield; his place was taken by another veteran in the Ripper hunt, Detective Chief Superintendent Holland.

"Ripper letters" continued to arrive at Oldfield's desk and the police were more than ever convinced that they were genuine. Forensic evidence had shown that the murderer was a person with the rare blood group B; it was now established, from saliva tests on the stamps, that the letter-writer had the same blood group.

Tapes and Number Plates

After the letters came the tapes. Detectives were able to hear the voice of the man they thought was the killer, a controlled, chilling voice with a north-east accent. It promised that the Ripper would strike again.

Four more times the Ripper struck. Barbara Leach, a student, and Marguerite Wallis, a civil servant, were murdered; two more women escaped from attacks. On 17 November, 1980, Jacqueline Hill, a 20 year-old student, was killed within sight of her lodgings on Alma Road, Leeds. She was the Ripper's last victim.

On the evening of 3 January, 1981, two police officers making a routine patrol of the red-light area of Sheffield questioned the occupants of a Rover car which bore false

BELOW
Marilyn Moore, one of the women fortunate enough to escape the Ripper. On 14 December, 1977, Sutcliffe savagely attacked her with a **hammer on waste ground and left her for dead. Despite terrible injuries, she managed to stagger as far as a telephone box and give a description of her attacker.**

BELOW
Copies of letters were supposedly written by the Ripper and sent to police via various **national newspapers. Like the tapes, they were a hoax — but the man who wrote them might have been** **responsible for other killings originally attributed to the Ripper. Police are still searching for him.**

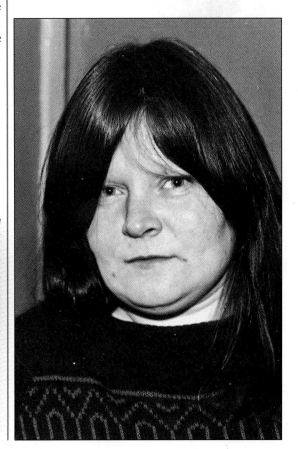

Daily Mail

SATURDAY, MAY 23, 1981

12p

SUTCLIFFE GUILTY OF 13 MURDERS WILL GO TO PRISON FOR LIFE, AND THAT IS WHAT IT MEANS

THEY'LL NEVER LET HIM OUT

One-way journey to a life behind bars

The Yorkshire Ripper is a sadistic sex murderer, not a madman, a jury decided yesterday. Now he will almost certainly be locked up for the rest of his life.

Peter Sutcliffe, 34, killed 13 women and brutally attacked seven more for pleasure — not because he had a mission from God after a graveyard 'miracle' involving a talking tombstone.

That was rejected by the Old Bailey jurors as so many lies he invented to fool four leading psychiatrists into diagnosing him as a paranoid schizophrenic.

Immediately the verdicts were announced, Attorney-General Sir Michael Havers QC, rose to his feet and said : 'The prognosis is that in the view of the doctors, this man should be locked up for the rest of his life.'

Dr Terence Kay, one of two forensic psychiatrists who were briefed by the Crown, was recalled to the witness box. He said : 'In the light of the present knowledge of the illness of schizophrenia, we believe that he should be kept in custody for the rest of his natural life.'

Then the judge, Mr Justice Boreham, sentenced the man who terrorised the North of England for five and a half years to 20

By HARRY LONGMUIR and IAN SMITH

concurrent life terms of imprisonment, with a recommendation to the Home Secretary that he should serve at least 30 years.

He told Sutcliffe : 'That is a long period, an unusually long period in my judgment, but you, I believe, are an unusually dangerous man.'

He added : 'I express the hope that, when I have said life imprisonment, it will mean precisely that.'

Afterwards Sutcliffe's wife Sonia said in an interview with the Star newspaper in

Sheffield : 'Of course I'm standing by him. I still love him.'

She intended to see him as often as she could.

'I know that he is going away for a long, long time,' she said. 'But I don't want to look too far ahead. How can you say what is going to happen in a few years or even today?'

As for herself, she said she thought that some people 'might try to get at me. I can accept that and if it happens—it happens. There's not much I can do about it.'

'I've never thought of taking a new identity. But I don't know about changing my name because I've never used my married name much.'

As for the question that has been asked all over Britain—and she has answered to the total satisfaction of the police—did she know ? She repeated again that of course she did not.

She found out, she said, when she went to Dewsbury police station after her husband's arrest.

'There were several policemen in the room when he came in. He nodded his head and said 'It's me love.' I couldn't believe it because he had behaved so normally at home.'

Since the trial began Sonia Sutcliffe has spoken to her husband only twice. 'He seems to be bearing up quite well,' she said. 'But I

Turn to Page 2, Col 1

Full coverage—Pages 2, 3, 4, 6 and 7

Peter Sutcliffe, whose killings terrified millions of women

INSIDE : Foreign News 10, TV Guide 17-24, Gardening 26, 27, City 28, 29, Letters 32, Prize Crossword 33, Quick Crossword 37, Sport 33-40

number plates. Inside were a prostitute and a man called Peter Sutcliffe.

Sutcliffe, a native of Bradford and a lorry driver, was a married man living with his attractive wife, Sonia. He was taken to a Sheffield police station and held in custody. On 5 January, 1981, he was brought to Dewsbury Magistrate's Court to be charged on two counts. The first was the theft of two number plates. The second was that "between the 16th and 19th November, 1980,

you did murder Jacqueline Hill".

At his trial Peter Sutcliffe, 35 years old, the eldest of six children, admitted the murder of 13 women and the attempted murder of seven more. Psychiatrists could find no evidence to show that he was insane. He was sentenced to life imprisonment, with a recommendation that he should serve no less than 30 years.

CHARLES MANSON AND HIS "FAMILY"

TOP
The four members of the "family" who carried out the Sharon Tate murders at Manson's bidding: Patricia Krenwinkel, Charles Watson, Susan Atkins and Linda Kasabian. It was Susan Atkins who provided the vital testimony that led to conviction.

RIGHT
Charles Manson, head of the "family" whose hatred of almost everything, including themselves, drove them to commit terrible crimes. Manson, 34 years old, had spent half his life in prison. He exerted a strange magnetic influence on his "disciples".

INSET
Jay Sebring, an internationally known hairdresser, who was one of the victims. He bled to death from seven stab wounds and one gunshot wound. Sebring, 35, was Sharon Tate's former lover.

RIGHT
The fashionable home in Benedict Canyon, Beverly Hills, that was the scene of the Sharon Tate murders. Four members of the Manson gang broke into the house just after midnight on 9 August, 1969.

SCENE OF MULTIPLE SL

No one will ever know what dark worms crawl in the recesses of Peter Sutcliffe's mind, whether it was a hatred of prostitutes, or some deeper, underlying hatred that drove him to commit his hideous crimes. But it was hatred pure and simple, hatred of almost everything, including themselves, that motivated Charles Manson and the group of people he called his "Family".

Just after midnight on 9 August, 1969, four members of Manson's gang – three women and a man – broke into 10050 Cielo Drive, a fashionable house in Benedict Canyon, Beverly Hills, and brutally murdered its five occupants. This was the home of 26-year-old actress, Sharon Tate, and her husband, the film director Roman Polanski, who at the time was working in London.

The House-party Murders

Sharon's guests that night were Jay Sebring, 35 years old, a hair stylist and owner of a corporation known as Sebring International, who was her former lover; 25-year-old Abigail Folger, heiress to the Folger coffee empire; Abigail's lover, Wojiciech "Voytek" Frykowski, a drug addict who lived off the Folger fortune; and Steven Earl Parent, 18 years old, a recent high-school graduate who worked as a delivery boy.

Sharon Tate died from multiple stab wounds to the chest and back that penetrated the heart, lungs and liver, causing massive haemorrhage. She was stabbed 16 times.

Jay Sebring bled to death from seven stab wounds and one gunshot wound.

Abigail Folger died from 28 stab wounds to the body.

"Voytek" Frykowski was stabbed 51 times, shot twice, and struck over the head 13 times with a blunt instrument.

Steven Earl Parent died as a result of four gunshot wounds.

Only Sharon Tate and Jay Sebring were found dead in the house. Steven Parent died at the wheel of his car; the bodies of Voytek Frykowski and Abigail Folger were found on the lawn not far from the front door. None of the victims had been tortured or sexually molested.

There was more. On Sunday, 10 August, Leno LaBianca, the president of a Los Angeles supermarket chain, and his wife,

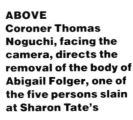

ABOVE
Coroner Thomas Noguchi, facing the camera, directs the removal of the body of Abigail Folger, one of the five persons slain at Sharon Tate's home. In the foreground is the sheet-covered body of "Voytek" Frykowski, who had been stabbed 31 times, shot twice and struck over the head 13 times.

Rosemary, were murdered at 3301 Waverly Drive, their home in the Los Feliz district of the city. Leno had been stabbed 12 times and his body also had four puncture wounds made by a double-tined fork. His wife had been stabbed 41 times. Despite the similarities between the Tate and LaBianca killings, police saw no reason to link the two. Detectives drew up a list of suspects. One of them was Charles Manson.

Manson, a 34-year-old ex-convict who had spent half his life in prison, was already in police custody. So were 24 members of his "Family". Most had been arrested during a raid on the Barker Ranch, their hideout in the Death Valley National Monument. The charges against them ranged from grand theft to arson. Two were charged with the murder of a music teacher, Gary Hinman.

The woman in question was Susan Atkins, 21, also known by the "Family" name of Sadie Mae Glutz. On 6 November she confessed to a cellmate that she had murdered Sharon Tate and that three members of the Manson Family had killed the LaBiancas. The cellmate decided to tell the police.

A Hippy Gang

The Manson Family was a product of San Francisco, a city where, in the late 1960s, free food, music, dope, love and the preachings of self-styled gurus were all there for the asking. Manson had gone there in 1967, having recently been released from prison. In his own words, "we slept in the park and we lived on the streets and my hair got a little longer and I started playing music and

> ## "We slept in the park and we lived on the streets"

people liked my music and people smiled at me and put their arms around me and hugged me – I didn't know how to act. It just took me away. It grabbed me up, man, that there were people that are real."

One of the "real people" was 23-year-old Mary Brunner, a librarian. She was not attractive; Manson cultivated her and, eventually, moved in with her. She was the first of the Family.

Before long there were 18, mostly girls, but also a few young boys. Manson, barely five feet two inches tall, exercised a mesmeric hold over them. Locked inside their hazy world of sex, drugs and music, they would do anything for him. Even kill.

It was not until detectives taped a lengthy interview with Susan Atkins that investigators knew, for the first time, who had been involved in the Tate and LaBianca killings. Manson had not gone along himself. Those who did go were Charles "Tex" Watson, Susan Atkins, Patricia Krenwinkel and Linda Kasabian. The next night, Manson entered the home of Leno and Rosemary LaBianca and tied them up. He then sent in Watson, Krenwinkel and a girl named Leslie Van Houten to murder them.

By 5 December, 1969, the prosecution took the Tate and LaBianca cases before the Los Angeles County grand jury. After hearing the icy, dispassionate testimony of Susan Atkins, the jury returned indictments: Leslie Van Houten, two counts of murder and one of conspiracy to commit murder; Charles Manson, Charles Watson, Patricia Krenwinkel, Susan Atkins and Linda Kasabian, seven counts of murder and one of conspiracy to commit murder.

ABOVE
Sharon Tate's husband, Roman Polanski, the celebrated film director. On the night of the murders Polanski was working in London.

RIGHT
Charles Manson on his way to court in Los Angeles. According to some sources, the Manson family murdered no fewer than 45 people before it was broken up. The true figure may never be known.

ABOVE
Members of the jury that found Manson and his three female co-defendants guilty of first-degree murder leave the courthouse for their bus under heavy guard. The defendants were sentenced to death, but this was later reduced to life imprisonment.

ABOVE
Four women members of the Manson "family", their heads shaven, kneel on the sidewalk outside the Los Angeles Hall of Justice. They kept vigil throughout the long trial in which Manson and his accomplices were convicted of murder.

There was still a long way to go before the defendants could be brought to trial. The prosecution needed evidence to corroborate Susan Atkins' testimony; above all, they needed to establish a motive for the killings. Atkins herself provided an answer of sorts.

"Judgment Day"

"The whole thing," she told Prosecutor Vincent Bugliosi, "was done to instil fear in the establishment and cause paranoia. Also to show the black man how to take over the white man." It was intended to be the start of "Helter Skelter" – an expression that had been written in blood on a wall of the LaBianca house. It meant the same as Judgment Day, Armageddon. "There was a so-called motive behind all this," she stated. "It was to instil fear into the pigs and bring on judgment day, which is here now for all."

For Charles Manson and his accomplices, judgment day came on 19 April, 1971. After a trial lasting nine and a half months, they were sentenced to death. In 1972, when California abolished the death penalty, the sentences were reduced to life imprisonment.

According to some sources, the Manson Family murdered no fewer than 45 people before it was broken up. The true figure may never be known.

Manson and Girls Get Death

MYRA HINDLEY AND IAN BRADY:

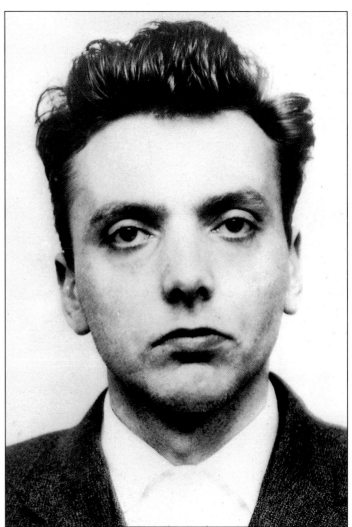

THE "MOORS MURDERERS"

On 23 November, 1963, John Kilbride, aged 12, set out from his home in Ashton-under-Lyne, on the outskirts of Greater Manchester, to go to a cinema matinée. Afterwards, he visited the local market with a friend and then the two went their separate ways, John setting out in the gathering darkness to walk to the bus station. He was never seen alive again.

Thirteen months later, on 26 December, 1964, Lesley Ann Downey, aged 10, left her home in Ancoats, also in Greater Manchester, to visit a Christmas fun fair with her two brothers and some friends. In the jostle of the crowd, she became separated from the others. She was last seen standing by the merry-go-round, gazing in fascination.

On 6 October, 1965, Edward Evans, aged 17, set out on a pub crawl from his home in Ardwick, a couple of miles from the Downey residence. His last port of call was the Central Station Buffet.

"Help him! Help him!"

At 11.40 that evening, David and Maureen Smith were awakened in their Manchester home by the ringing of the doorbell. At the door was Maureen's 23-year-old sister, Myra Hindley. She said that she had come to leave a message for their mother. Myra had recently moved into a neighbouring street, Wardle Brook Avenue, with her boyfriend, Ian Brady, who worked as a stock clerk in the same firm where she was a typist. She said that she was afraid to walk back in the dark; would Dave Smith go with her?

Arriving at 16 Wardle Brook Avenue, Dave was invited by Brady into the kitchen. Brady went upstairs, came back down with three miniature bottles of brandy, and then went into the sitting-room.

A few moments later, Smith heard a piercing scream, followed by a cry from Myra: "Dave, help him! Help him!"

Smith dashed into the other room and stood frozen in disbelief. Writhing on the floor was a screaming figure. Brady stood astride it, striking it again and again with an axe. Fifteen times the axe came down. Blood spattered the walls. The screams gave way to gurgles and moans. Then there was silence.

To one side stood Myra Hindley, motionless, watching with dull eyes, like a woman in a trance.

In a state of deep shock, not really comprehending what he had witnessed, Smith helped Brady and Hindley to clear up the mess and to carry the lifeless, battered corpse into Myra's bedroom. Then they all had a cup of tea together.

At 3 am Smith rose to leave. Calmly, Brady saw him to the front door and said goodnight. Smith ran all the way home and told the tale to his incredulous wife. She told her husband to call the police. At 8.40 am, a team of police under Superintendent Robert Talbot arrived at the house in Wardle Brook Avenue, where they found Evans' body. Brady and Hindley were taken into custody.

Saddleworth Moor

On 8 October, 1965, Ian Brady was charged with the murder of Edward Evans at Hyde Police Court. As he left the dock he nodded at a blonde woman. The blonde was Myra Hindley, who had earlier been released; the police had no evidence of her complicity in the murder.

Meanwhile, Detective Chief Superintendent Arthur Benfield had been going through documents found at 16 Wardle Brook Avenue. Among them was what

Inside the suitcase were photographs

appeared to be a detailed plan for disposing of a human body. There was also a list of names, scrawled in Brady's handwriting. One name struck a chord in Benfield's memory: the name of John Kilbride. And there were also photographs of moorland – lots of them.

ABOVE
The house at No. 16, Wardle Brook Avenue, Manchester, where Brady and Hindley lived. It was here that they made tape recordings and took photographs of the agony of their child victims. One tape recorded the terrified pleas for mercy of Lesley Ann Downey.

LEFT
Edward Evans, the 17-year-old battered to death by Brady on 6 October, 1965. The brutal killing was witnessed by Dave Smith, Myra Hindley's brother-in-law. Fearful of Brady, Smith drank tea at the murder house before rushing off to raise the alarm.

That, Benfield was convinced, was where the search for John Kilbride must begin. With the help of Dave Smith, they isolated areas of moorland known to have been visited by Brady, areas that matched the photographs. The search was narrowed down to lonely Saddleworth Moor. There, on 16 October, 1965, searchers probing an area of waterlogged peat came upon the partly exposed body of a child – the body, not of John Kilbride, but of Lesley Ann Downey.

Among Myra Hindley's possessions detectives found a left-luggage ticket. It led them to a suitcase. Inside it were photographs: harrowing pictures of a naked child, gagged with a scarf, her eyes terrified and pleading. The child was Lesley Ann Downey. The detectives found something else – a tape, recording Lesley Ann's pleas for mercy, her terrified whimperings, her entreaties to be sent home to her mother.

There was no longer any doubt about Hindley's part in this terror. Her voice, too, was on the tape.

On Thursday, 21 October 1965, what was left of little John Kilbride was found lying in the same moor that had concealed the remains of Lesley Ann Downey.

Throughout their trial at Chester Assizes, which lasted from 19 April until 6 May, 1966, Brady and Hindley persisted in a "not guilty" plea to all three murders. Ian Brady was found guilty of all three, Myra Hindley of the murders of Lesley Ann Downey and Edward Evans. To the murder of John Kilbride, Hindley was found guilty of being an accessory after the fact. Both were sentenced to life imprisonment. They are still in prison today.

A Macabre Postscript

After all these years psychiatrists are still trying to unravel the mind of Ian Brady, to uncover the springs of action that led to the motiveless torture and killing of innocents. Hindley, obsessed by him, as the girls of the Manson Family were obsessed by their leader, did his bidding without question. As

BELOW
Behind protective screens, police recover the body of a victim. The body of John Kilbride was found in October, 1965, not far from where Lesley Ann Downey had been buried.

her diary revealed, she was utterly under his spell from the moment she met him.

There is a postscript. On 16 June, 1964, a 12-year-old schoolboy, Keith Bennett, went missing in the Greater Manchester area. His disappearance followed that of 16-year-old Pauline Reade, who failed to return home from a visit to a social club on 12 July, 1963. A massive police search revealed no trace of either youngster.

But in July, 1987, detectives found another body in a remote trace of Saddleworth Moor. It lay in a shallow grave only yards from where Lesley Ann Downey had been found. The discovery came after Myra Hindley, having herself come forward with more information about the 23-year-old killings, returned with police to the windswept moor. The body was never positively identified, but it was thought to be that of Pauline Reade.

While Hindley was on her second escorted visit to the moor, police apprehended a man who, armed with a knife, sought to kill her. He was Pat Kilbride, the father of John. The relatives of the victims have long and bitter memories.

ABOVE
The face of a killer. Ian Brady, smoking a cigarette and accompanied by a uniformed policeman, on his way to the court in Hyde, Cheshire, in October, 1965, to be charged with the murder of Edward Evans. Police at first could find no evidence of Myra Hindley's complicity in the murder.

LEFT
The Moors Murders charge hearing was held at Hyde, in Cheshire. The photograph shows David Smith and his wife Maureen, key witnesses in the case, leaving the courtroom. Maureen Smith was Hindley's sister.

ABOVE
Detective Chief Inspector John Tyrell, of Manchester City police, one of the senior officers who conducted the inquiry into the Moors Murders. Others were Detective Chief Superintendent Arthur Benfield and Superintendent Robert Talbot, who found Evans' body.

THE UNSOLVED CASE OF JACK THE RIPPER

In the league table of serial killers, Jack the Ripper does not rate very highly. He killed five women – all prostitutes – in a 10-week period from 31 August to 9 November, 1888, although four other murders that year may also have been his work.

He stalked the Whitechapel area of London, killing all but one of his victims while they were soliciting on the streets. The last of his certain victims, Mary Kelly, was murdered in her room after escorting the Ripper there.

The Ripper's attack was so swift and violent that the women had no time to make a sound. Their throats were slashed with such force that they were nearly decapitated.

Their breasts were hacked off and their vaginas, ovaries and uterus cut out with surgical skill. Their intestines were sometimes thrown over their right shoulder, reminiscent, some people thought, of a Masonic rite.

Jack the Ripper gave himself his own grim name in taunting letters that he wrote to the police. In one of them he enclosed half of a victim's kidney. Despite a massive police effort, however, he was never found. Two murderers confessed to Jack's crimes on the way to the

BELOW
Hanbury Street, Spitalfields, London, where the mutilated body of Annie Chapman was found in a backyard on 8 September, 1888. She was probably the most hopeless and helpless of all Jack the Ripper's victims. The mother of three children, she had been married to a veterinary surgeon, but the family was broken up by her alcoholism and she eventually became a prostitute.

LEFT
Engraving from the *Illustrated Police News*, 1889, showing gallant members of the public tackling a villainous-looking Jack the Ripper as he pounces on another victim. In all probability, the man who stalked the streets of Whitechapel was as respectably dressed as the gentleman in the bowler hat.

gallows, but it is unlikely that either of them was responsible.

Theories abound. Everyone from the local kosher butchers to Prince "Eddy", Albert Victor, the bisexual Duke of Clarence and heir to the throne who died of syphilis, has been suspected. James K. Stephen, a homosexual poet, exiled Russian aristocratic psychopaths, a local cobbler and the Queen's physician have all been suggested. But the favourite candidate is Montague J. Druitt, a surgeon who drowned himself in the Thames shortly after the last murder was discovered.

GUNPOWDER, TREASON AND PLOT

"Assassination," George Bernard Shaw wrote, "is the extreme form of censorship." Like high treason, it proceeds from political motives. And for that very reason moral judgement of both the assassin and the traitor often hangs suspended.

THE STRANGE CASE OF "LORD HAW HAW"

It was 26 September, 1939, and the Second World War was just three weeks old. Shortly after 11 am, a German reconnaissance aircraft sighted a British naval force in the North Sea. It consisted of two battleships, two battle cruisers, three light cruisers – and the aircraft carrier, HMS *Ark Royal*.

The *Ark Royal* was the Royal Navy's latest and most powerful carrier. It was attacked by Junkers Ju 88 dive bombers, whose pilots reported several near-misses and what appeared to be a direct hit on the bows.

The next evening a sinister voice, broadcasting in strongly accented English from a German radio station, crackled over the air waves. "We have an important communication for listeners," it said. "Where is the *Ark Royal*? It was hit in a German attack on 26 September at 3 pm. There was a terrific explosion. Where is the *Ark Royal*? Britain, ask your Admiralty."

The British Admiralty countered with a dry announcement which stated that the *Ark Royal* had returned to base. The English-speaking German announcer labelled this a trick to camouflage "heavy losses". But at the beginning of October there came news which shattered the German propaganda. The *Ark Royal* was at sea again, taking part in the hunt for the German battleship *Admiral Graf Spee*, in the Atlantic.

LEFT
HMS *Ark Royal*, the British aircraft carrier which Lord Haw-Haw claimed the Germans had sunk several times over in the early months of the war. It was not until November 1941 that she went to the bottom in the Mediterranean, victim of a U-boat's torpedo.

ABOVE LEFT
William Joyce, alias Lord Haw-Haw, pictured behind his desk at a German radio station. The road to treason began with his involvement with the British Fascist movement in the mid 1920s. A scuffle left him with a knife scar across his right cheek.

The owner of the voice which had alleged the destruction of the *Ark Royal* in September, 1939, had been broadcasting since the beginning of the war, always prefixing his comments with the words "Germany calling, Germany calling". He placed emphasis on the first syllable of the name Germany, so that it sounded more like "Jairmany". Throughout the war, it was to be a kind of identifying trademark.

"Germany calling, Germany calling"

On 14 September, 1939, a *Daily Express* columnist writing under the pseudonym Jonah Barrington, made this observation: "A gent I'd like to meet is moaning periodically from Zeesen [one of the main German radio transmitters]. He speaks English of the haw-haw, damit-get-out-of-my-way variety, and his strong suit is gentlemanly indignation." A few days later, the *Daily Express* announced: "Jonah Barrington, listening at the *Daily Express* short wave station to the war on the radio, introduces 'Lord Haw-Haw'."

And so Lord Haw-Haw he became to the millions of Britons who, anxious for news of the war, tuned in to German radio broadcasts as well as those of the BBC.

ABOVE RIGHT
The Humbug of Hamburg, as William Joyce was described by the *Sunday Graphic* of 17 March, 1940. Although most Britons treated Haw-Haw with derision, his lies caused considerable anxiety among the families of British servicemen who were serving overseas.

RIGHT
The British Fascist leader was Sir Oswald Mosley. He was imprisoned during the war for his activities, but tried to resurrect the movement after Germany's defeat. He is seen here speaking at a Fascist conference in 1948.

THE TRAITOR'S MORAL DILEMMA

Why do people betray their country? The answer, most commonly, is for money or to escape blackmail. At the height of the Cold War, the Soviet security police, the KGB, used blackmail as a primary weapon, luring western government officials into compromising situations and then threatening them with public exposure if they failed to co-operate.

On the other hand, many people have committed so-called acts of betrayal because they genuinely believed that what they were doing was right. One such was Klaus Fuchs, the son of a German Protestant pastor. Fuchs had fled from the Nazis and in 1944 was assigned to the Manhattan Project in the United States that was developing the atom bomb. In 1945 he passed on everything he knew about the bomb to a Soviet agent known as Raymond, alias Harry Cold, because he believed that the awesome secrets of Armageddon should not be the property of one nation alone.

It was not until 1950 that Fuchs confessed what he had done. By that time the Soviet Union had detonated its first atomic device. In the United States anti-Communist sentiment had been gathering momentum and the hunt for traitors was on. Early in August, 1948, the Un-American Activities Committee had set in motion one of the most sensational cases of the post-war decade, when Alger Hiss, a former member of the Roosevelt administration, was accused of having belonged to the Communist Party in the 1930s and of having passed secret documents to Soviet agents in Washington. Hiss denied the

charges, but was found guilty of perjury in January, 1950. One of his main prosecutors became something of a national hero: his name was Richard Nixon.

Fuchs' confession in the following month, set the stage for the entrance of Senator Joseph McCarthy. He entered the Senate in 1947 and for three years went largely unnoticed – until he decided to turn the Communist issue to his advantage. McCarthy claimed to have in his possession a list of no fewer than 205 employees of the State Department who were known to be Communist Party members.

This charge was not substantiated, but McCarthy rode high on a wave of popular hysteria until he was discredited by the army hearings of 1954. Among his notable targets was Dr J. Robert Oppenheimer, who had directed the construction of the atomic bomb during the Second World War and had since become the US government's principal adviser on nuclear policy. On the flimsiest evidence, Oppenheimer was judged to be a major security risk and was suspended from his post.

LEFT
J. Robert Oppenheimer and his wife pictured in Athens. This brilliant scientist, who had directed the construction of the atomic bomb in World War II, fell victim to the anti-communist witch hunts that took place in the United States during the 1950s.

BELOW
Klaus Fuchs, on the left, seen at London Airport on his way to East Berlin. Fuchs passed on everything he knew about the atomic bomb to Soviet agents because he genuinely believed that the awesome weapon should not be the property of one nation alone.

An Irish Upbringing

His real name was William Joyce. He was born of an Irish father and English mother in the United States in 1906. He went to Ireland with his parents in 1909, was educated at Catholic schools, and was brought up in a household that was fervently loyal to the British Crown. His father suffered for his pro-British stance in the Irish rebellion of 1916, having much of his property burned. In 1920, as the situation in Ireland worsened, young William sought revenge by becoming a youthful informer for the para-military Auxiliaries, the hated "Black and Tans".

In December, 1921, Michael Joyce took his family to England. William, although not yet 16, joined the regular Army; he gave his age as 18, explaining that he had never been issued with a birth certificate. His Army career, however, was short-lived; his real age was discovered when he was admitted to hospital with rheumatic fever and he was discharged after serving only four months.

In 1923 Joyce entered London University, where he joined the Officer Training Corps.

Someone tried to cut his throat with a razor

A year later he became involved in the embryonic British Fascist movement. In October, 1924, during a scuffle with what he later called "Jewish Communists" at the Lambeth Baths Hall in southeast London, someone tried to cut his throat with a razor. Joyce's woollen scarf saved his life, but he was slashed across the right cheek from the corner of his mouth to behind his ear. The resulting scar marred his handsome features and gave him a sinister appearance that enhanced his tough reputation on the political platform.

By the early 1930s Joyce was heavily involved with the British Union of Fascists, led by Sir Oswald Mosley. But the Fascist cause made little headway in Great Britain and in 1939, as the clouds of war gathered, Joyce and his second wife, Margaret, emigrated to Germany.

Trapped in Berlin

The Joyces arrived in Berlin, with British passports, on 27 August, 1939. Four days later Germany invaded Poland. It was then that Joyce received a shock. A friend told him that if war broke out between Great Britain and Germany, he and his wife would be separated and interned.

John Angus McNab (left) Joyce's former lieutenant in the B.U.F., talks with Michael Edge-Egan, a South African friend of Joyce. On the right is Quintin Joyce brother of "Lord Haw-Haw." All three attended the trial at the Old Bailey

Joyce may go into the witness box today

"Daily Mirror" Reporter

WILLIAM JOYCE may go into the witness box to give evidence in his own defence when the treason trial is continued at the Old Bailey today.

The decision whether or not to call Joyce was being made last night.

There will be at least seven witnesses for the defence.

Joyce was jaunty and smiling when he went into the dock yesterday to plead not guilty to the indictment.

In the crowded public gallery were four young men whom Joyce seemed to recognise as friends. He turned to them once, smiled, and raised his right hand in greeting.

The four were dressed in black. Two wore black pullovers with high roll collars, one a black scarf and one a black bow tie.

Joyce sat unconcernedly, hands folded, while a legal battle developed between counsel for the prosecution and defence on his nationality.

Mr. G. O. Slade, K.C., for Joyce, based his case on one main point: "I am hoping to prove that William Joyce has never been a British subject at any time throughout his life."

After Mr. Justice Tucker had told Mr. Slade: "There is some evidence which, if uncontradicted, would entitle the jury to come to the conclusion that this man is a British subject," the defence opened their case.

It was that on October 25, 1894, Mr. Michael Joyce—the prisoner's father—became a naturalised citizen of America. On a trip to this country Michael Joyce became engaged to a girl in Shaw, Lancs, and married her in New York on May 2, 1905.

William Joyce was born 11 months later. Mr. Slade made his point—Joyce could not be English.

To prove this the defence had had flown from America a sealed and certified copy of the U.S. naturalisation record showing the Michael Joyce entry.

When the Court adjourned Joyce bowed stiffly, correctly, to Mr. Justice Tucker and with precise military strides left the dock.

Joyce at once made plans to return to England. He tried to buy two railway tickets with Reichsmarks – only to be told that German currency was not acceptable for a journey outside Germany. An official at the British Consulate listened politely to Joyce's dilemma, but said that he was unable to help.

In desperation, Joyce turned for advice to Margaret, who said that they might as well stay where they were. It was business-as-usual in Berlin; life was relaxed and normal; food and drink were plentiful. But, she pointed out, their small store of money would not last for ever. Joyce would have to find a job.

Joyce, who was fluent in German, found a temporary job as a translator, but it did not bring in enough money to support them. He tried the German Foreign Office; and an official there suggested that an English speaker, especially one faithful to Fascist ideals, might come in useful at the *Reichs-rundfunk*, the German Radio Corporation.

The head of the corporation's overseas short-wave services, Walter Kamm, had already assembled a small team of Anglo-German newsreaders and commentators. Joyce accepted an invitation to join the team. He was desperate for money and here was work in which he could put his powers of oratory to good use.

ABOVE
As the *Daily Mirror* reported, Lord Haw-Haw's trial was attended by J. A. McNab (left), Joyce's former lieutenant in the British Union of Fascists, and Quintin Joyce (right), brother of the accused.

★ Joyce—stretcher case ★

Seen with some of his guards is the traitor, lying on a stretcher in the motor ambulance him to the British General Hospital after his Second Army Headquarters.

Joyce read his first news bulletin on 11 September, 1939. The text is not recorded. It was only with the *Ark Royal* incident that British authorities began to take notice of the new English-speaking voice that pronounced "Germany" with a peculiar intonation. (Joyce's slightly nasal twang was the legacy of an untreated broken nose, acquired during a schoolboy fight in Ireland.)

It was not long before the voice of "Lord Haw-Haw", with its insidious tones, became the most hated – and the most fascinating – to emanate from German radio. Joyce seemed to have an uncanny knowledge of Allied movements; he knew the names of British personalities and politely enquired about their welfare.

"Good morning, rats. Have you emerged from your holes yet, rats?"

In the summer of 1941, when British Commonwealth troops were fighting desperately against General Rommel's Afrika Korps in North Africa, he broadcast: "Good morning, rats. Have you emerged from your holes yet, rats? How are you this morning, and how is your Air Force? Oh, I forgot, you haven't got one, have you? Never mind, we'll send you some planes . . ." And so the "Desert Rats" were born.

The British authorities were worried about Joyce's contribution to the German propaganda effort. He was clever; he would single out a munitions factory in some English town and ask casually over the radio "how Mrs Betty Smith was getting on". The odds were that there would be a Mrs Betty Smith somewhere among the workforce. Touches such as these hinted that he had an army of agents and informers in England.

By 1943 it was becoming increasingly difficult to extol Germany's victories. The RAF and USAAF were hammering Germany's cities by night and day; the Axis effort in North Africa had collapsed; and the German Sixth Army had been annihilated at Stalingrad. As 1944 opened, everyone knew that it would be the invasion year. The Germans scoffed at the possibility of a successful Allied landing in Europe. "What British politician wants to hear of Poland today?" Joyce demanded derisively, reminding British soldiers that they had been asked to die to preserve Poland's integrity. Now hundreds of thousands of British and American soldiers were "to die for the Jewish policy of Stalin and Roosevelt".

ABOVE LEFT
The end for the Germans in Africa, March, 1943. "Desert Rats" escort German prisoners taken in the battle for the Mareth Line in Tunisia, where Axis troops made their last stand against General Bernard Montgomery's Eighth Army.

ABOVE RIGHT
Seen with his guards, William Joyce is shown lying wounded on a stretcher in the motor ambulance which transported him to a British Army hospital in Germany.

BELOW
The notice that was pinned on the gates of Wandsworth Prison, London, on the morning of 3 January, 1946, announcing that William Joyce had been found guilty of high treason and duly executed by hanging. To the last, he remained unrepentant.

HAW-HAW, TO BE RE-BURIED IN EIRE

LORD HAW-HAW, William Joyce, who broadcast Nazi propaganda to Britain in the 1939-45 war, is to reburied in Eire in November, it was disclosed yesterday.

The civic authorities at Galway, where Joyce spent his childhood, are allowing the burial, following the Home Office's authorisation of his exhumation from the cemetery at Wandsworth Prison, where he was hanged in 1946.

The burial follows a 10-year battle by Joyce's daughter, Mrs Heather Iandolo, a Gillingham, schoolteacher, to get his body returned to Ireland.

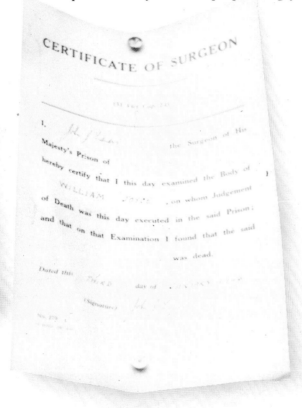

CERTIFICATE OF SURGEON

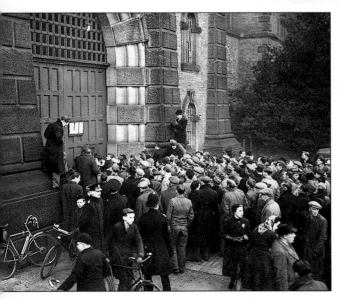

LEFT
Crowds gathered outside Wandsworth Prison read the notice of Joyce's execution. His widow, Margaret, was interned in Germany, but regained her British nationality and died in London in 1972.

Unrepentant to the End

But in June, 1944, the invasion came. By April, 1945, Berlin lay in ruins and the Propaganda Ministry's English Language Service moved to Apen, a small town between Bremen and the Dutch frontier. Joyce, who had joined the *Volkssturm*, the German Home Guard, was dismayed by the move; he had made up his mind that he would die fighting in the rubble of Berlin.

Joyce made his last broadcast to Britain on 30 April, 1945, the day on which Hitler committed suicide:

Britain's victories are barren. They leave her poor and they leave her people hungry. They leave her bereft of the markets and the wealth that she possessed six years ago. But, above all, they leave her with an immensely greater problem than she had then. We are nearing the end of one phase in Europe's history, but the next will be no happier. It will be grimmer, harder and perhaps bloodier. And now I ask you earnestly, can Britain survive? I am profoundly convinced that without German help she cannot.

On the orders of Josef Goebbels, the German Propaganda Minister, tentative plans had been laid to spirit the Joyces out of Germany; but Goebbels died in Berlin and the plans came to nothing. They tried to escape to Sweden via Denmark, but Allied forces had landed ahead of them and they were forced to turn back. The end of the war found them in the village of Kupfermühle, near the Danish border; their apartment was visited several times by British soldiers, who took them for an ordinary German couple and showed no interest in them.

One morning, soon after Germany's capitulation, Joyce went for a walk in the woods. He stumbled upon two British officers who were gathering wood for a fire. He spoke to them in French and walked on. Their suspicions aroused, the officers followed him. One of them, Lieutenant Perry, an interpreter, called out: "You wouldn't happen to be William Joyce, would you?" Joyce reached into an inside pocket for his German passport. Perry, thinking that Joyce was reaching for a weapon, fired his revolver. The bullet passed through both thighs and Joyce fell to the ground.

He was taken to Lüneburg, where he spent time in hospital recovering from his wounds, and then to Brussels, where he was detained while the British Parliament passed the Treason Act 1945, which made treachery a capital offence. On 16 June he was flown to London and taken to Brixton Prison.

His trial began at the Old Bailey on 17 September, 1945. It was a complex business; much hinged on Joyce's possession of a British passport and his allegiance to the Crown. But the outcome was never seriously in doubt, and no one showed much surprise when the jury, after only 23 minutes, found him guilty of high treason.

Joyce was executed on 3 January, 1946. To the end, he remained unrepentant. After the execution, Margaret Joyce was interned in Germany while her status was debated. She died in London in 1972, having regained her British nationality.

THE TRAGEDY OF ROGER CASEMENT

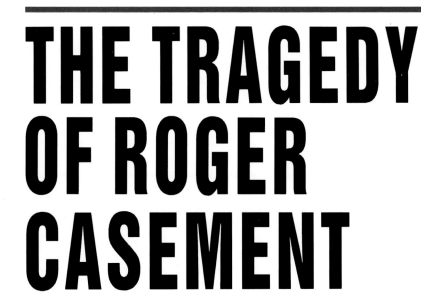

Roger David Casement was born on 1 September, 1864, into an Irish Protestant family at Sandycove, near Dublin, the youngest of four children. Both his parents died before he was 10, and the children were brought up by a guardian in Ulster, the Northern Ireland of today. Roger was always to think of himself as an Ulsterman.

On leaving school, Casement worked for a time as a clerk in a shipping line. The job was not to his liking and he soon abandoned it to work as an unpaid volunteer in the Congo, where the famous explorer, Henry

"Ireland, if she only knew, holds a winning hand between England and Germany"

Stanley, was charting the course of the Congo River. Later, he served for a time as British Consul in Lourenço Marques and St Paul de Loanda. In 1904 he presented a damning report on the ruthless exploitation of slave labour in the Congo Free State by Leopold II, King of the Belgians. Six years later, after a visit to the Upper Amazon, Casement provided another report, even more horrifying, on the maltreatment of natives in the Putumayo district by the British Peruvian Amazon Company.

The Ulster Volunteer

Casement's work for the British Colonial Service brought him a knighthood in 1911. In 1912 he visited Germany and was dis-

turbed by the growing rift between that country and Great Britain. In particular, he was concerned about Ireland's future role in European politics. Great Britain, he argued, had agreed to grant Home Rule to Ireland only to secure her as an ally against the Germans.

"The question arises," he wrote in the *Irish Review*, "could we not secure better terms? Would Germany offer us better? The more we value our own worth, the more others are likely to value it. Ireland, if she only knew, holds a winning hand between England and Germany."

Home Rule found little favour in Protestant-dominated Ulster, where a retired Army officer, Captain James Craig, formed the Ulster Volunteers, an armed militia dedicated to the defeat of "the present conspiracy to set up a Home Rule Parliament in Ireland" . . . and the winning of Irish inde-

ABOVE
Sir Roger Casement. The youngest of four children, he was born into an Irish Protestant family on 1 September, 1864. Despite what became of him, he was a loyal British subject – although his greater loyalty was to Ireland.

RIGHT
Sir Roger Casement, accompanied by a policeman, leaving the Law Courts in The Strand, London, in June, 1916. "It is not every day", he wrote, "that even an Irishman commits high treason — especially one who has been in the service of the Sovereign he discards, and not without honour and some fame in that service."

BELOW
Despite massive protests from friends and sympathizers, Casement was executed on 3 August, 1916. The photograph shows two associates, Mary Gorman and Martin Collins, on their way to Bow Street.

pendence. Casement became a member of the Ulster Volunteers' executive committee. He toured the country on a recruiting campaign, but quickly realized that it was not enough to secure recruits. "Had we only rifles and officers," he wrote, "we could have 150,000 splendid men in six months."

In the summer of 1914, thanks to the efforts of Casement and others, arms were obtained from sympathizers in the United States, although the shipment involved only 1,500 rifles of poor quality. The day after the arms reached Ireland, Austria declared war on Serbia and the First World War became a reality.

Casement was a Germanophile and from the outset his sympathies lay with Germany. "My heart bleeds for those poor people," her confided to a close friend. "They are beset by a world of hatred. Their crime is their efficiency."

Casement was in the United States when war broke out. He might have stayed there, for he no longer had any links with the British Foreign Service. But he was unhappy; there was not enough for him to do. In October, 1914, disguised as an American citizen named James Landy, with whom he swapped places, he sailed for Norway on the first stage of a journey that was to lead him to Berlin. He arrived in the German capital on the last day of the month.

Recruiting in Germany

His task, as he saw it, was three-fold: to secure German military aid for Ireland; to educate German public opinion on Ireland, so that the German people would support such action; and, if possible, to organize Irish prisoners-of-war into a military unit which would fight for Irish freedom.

On 20 November, 1914, the German Foreign Office announced that the "well-known Irish Nationalist, Sir Roger Casement," was in Berlin. It also issued a statement, on the order of the Chancellor, Theobold von Bethmann-Hollwegg, "that under no circumstances would Germany invade Ireland with a view to its conquest or the overthrow of any native institutions in that country". Should the war ever bring in its course German troops to the shores of Ireland, they would land there "as the forces of a Government that is inspired by goodwill towards a country and a people for whom Germany desires only national prosperity and national freedom".

This was a considerable coup and Casement pondered the possible consequences for himself. "It is not every day," he wrote in his diary, "that even an Irishman commits high treason – especially one who has been in the service of the Sovereign he discards, and not without honour and some fame in that service."

Casement's tour of the PoW camps in an effort to form an Irish Brigade for the nationalist cause was a disappointment. Most of the Irish prisoners had been captured in the retreat from Mons, and they had seen what the Germans had done to Belgium. They had no reason to believe that, if the Germans were to land in Ireland, their treatment of the Irish would be any different. Casement returned to Berlin despondent.

Renewed hope came in the spring of 1916. Irish nationalists were planning a rising, to take place at Easter, and the Germans had agreed to send a secret shipload of 20,000 rifles and ammunition. But the Germans were not prepared to provide officers to lead the rising, and Casement realized that without their expert assistance the insurgents would stand no chance against the disciplined British Army. He decided to return to Ireland to stop the rising.

The German authorities agreed to provide a submarine, the U-20, to take Casement to Ireland. Why they did this is not clear; it may be that they regarded him as a troublesome character and were eager to be rid of him. They were also, however, happy for the Irish rebellion to take place; it was doomed to failure, but it would cause trouble for the British. They therefore delayed the departure of the U-20 to ensure that Casement would not reach Ireland before the arms shipment, which was to be landed near

ABOVE
Sir Roger Casement in the dock at Bow Street Police Court with another prisoner, **Daniel Bailey. Casement, gaunt and thin, took copious notes of what was said.**

THE LAW OF TREASON

The laws covering treason in both Great Britain and the United States have their roots in the English Treason Act of 1351. It defined treason as (i) levying war against the government or supporting the enemies of the sovereign, (ii) plotting – or even imagining – the death of the sovereign, (iii) attempting to prevent the succession of rightful heirs to the throne or (iv) killing the Chancellor, Treasurer or the Sovereign's Justices while in the places doing their offices. It is also treason to "violate" the king's consort, his eldest unmarried daughter or the wife of his eldest son and heir.

In English law treason is one of the few offences that still carry a mandatory sentence of death by hanging. But in modern times prosecutions for treason have occurred only during wartime.

The framers of the American Constitution were naturally circumspect when it came to treason, since they had themselves committed treason – in British eyes – by taking up arms against George III. They also knew how easy it was to bring charges of treason against political opponents. They therefore denied Congress the right to change the law of treason once it had been written. Treason, against the United States is limited to "levying war against them, or in adhering to their enemies, giving them aid and comfort".

Laws of treason vary from country to country. In Japan, for example, since its defeat in the Second World War, it is treason to advocate war against another country or to try to frustrate alliances with other powers.

wave overturned the boat; they managed to clamber in again, but grounded the boat on a sandbank. When they finally reached the shore Casement, exhausted, took shelter in a rath – the remains of a Viking fort – while Monteith and the other man set out for Tralee, promising to return with a car.

It was the dinghy that gave Casement away. A passing policeman saw it tumbling in the breakers, investigated the rath and found Casement. Declining to believe his story that he was an English author who had been out for a stroll, he cautioned him and took him into custody.

On Easter Sunday Casement arrived in London. He was taken to Scotland Yard, where he made a full confession of his activities. He was imprisoned in the Tower. There he learned that the Easter Rising had failed and that its leaders had been captured and executed.

Tralee from a trawler on 20 April.

"The Bravest Man"

The U-20 reached Tralee Bay that night, but there was no sign of the trawler. Thanks to a navigational error it had made landfall several miles away. The U-Boat commander put Casement ashore and then made a run for the open sea before daylight.

Casement was placed in a dinghy with two other Irishmen who had made the voyage with him. One of them was Robert Monteith, a former officer in the Volunteers who had been sent to Germany to train the Irish Brigade. On their way to the shore, a

"He marched to the scaffold with the dignity of a prince"

In June, 1916, after a lengthy trial, Sir Roger Casement was found guilty of high treason and sentenced to death by hanging. Despite massive protests from friends, sympathizers and influential politicians, he was executed on 3 August, 1916. "He feared not death," wrote his priest, Father Carey; "he marched to the scaffold with the dignity of a prince." To Ellis, the hangman, Casement was "the bravest man it fell to my unhappy lot to execute".

THE ATTEMPTED ASSASSINATION OF POPE JOHN PAUL II

ABOVE
Pope John Paul II. On 13 May, 1981, the Pope was making one of his public appearances in St Peter's Square, Rome when a would-be assassin named Mehmet Ali Agca fired several shots at him. The Pope was badly wounded, but survived.

On 13 May, 1981, Pope John Paul II was making public appearances in St Peter's Square, Rome. Resplendent in his white robe, he was standing upright in a slow-moving jeep, conversing with the crowd, when several shots rang out. The Pope slumped, badly wounded; two tourists were also injured by stray bullets. In the ensuing panic, the crowd surged around the jeep. The man who had fired the shots tried to run, but was swept up in the mêlée and quickly seized by the Pope's bodyguard.

The would-be assassin was a Turk, named Mehmet Ali Agca. He was a fugitive from justice in his own country, where he was wanted for the murder of Abdi Ipekci, the editor of an Istanbul daily newspaper, *Milliyet*. He had escaped from a high-security prison in November, 1979, and had been on the run since.

Mehmet's escape from prison was made four days before Pope John Paul II was scheduled to visit Turkey. The day after, he called the offices of *Milliyet* and said that he had deposited a letter in a nearby mailbox. He was telling the truth.

The note read: "Western Imperialists, who fear that Turkey may establish a new Political, Military and Economic Force in the Middle East with brotherly Islamic countries, have rushed at a sensitive time to send Crusader Commander John Paul to Turkey under the guise of a religious leader. If this ill-timed and pointless visit is not cancelled, I will definitely shoot the pope. This is the only reason I escaped from prison."

A year and a half later, Agca carried out his threat. The Pope survived and Agca was subsequently sentenced to life imprisonment.

Agca was variously labelled as a left-wing extremist, a right-wing extremist, a religious fanatic and a madman. In fact, he appears to have been none of these. According to some suggestions, he may have been the agent of some power behind the scenes, a power that believed Pope John Paul II was taking too much of an active interest in world politics. There is a lot of evidence to show that Agca was motivated by some unseen force – but what that force might have been remains a mystery.

STALIN'S REVENGE:
THE MURDER OF
LEON TROTSKY

ABOVE
Trotsky pictured with newly graduated Red Army officers at the Soviet Military Academy, Moscow, in June, 1924. Trotsky, as commissar for war, was responsible for the triumph of the Russian Revolution against great odds.

Of the three great leaders of the Bolshevik revolution, Lenin, Trotsky and Stalin, Leon Trotsky remains perhaps the most enigmatic. Born in 1879, he was a Russian Jew and his real name was Lev Davidovich Bronstein; in his early revolutionary years he adopted the more Russian-sounding name of Trotsky, which he borrowed from a family that had belonged to the minor nobility in the reign of Ivan the Terrible.

As commissar for war, Trotsky was responsible for the triumph of the Russian Revolution and for its survival when 16 armies attempted to strangle the Soviet republic at birth. In 1921, when Lenin's "people's dictatorship" was revealed for what it really was – the dictatorship of a small, self-chosen, revolutionary elite – Trotsky issued the decrees to liquidate anyone who showed the slightest opposition to the regime.

Exile

On Lenin's death in 1924, however, Trotsky's star began to wane, and he found himself in opposition to the formidable Stalin, who held the army and the secret police in the palm of his hand. Barely escaping with their lives, Trotsky and his family were forced into exile, first in Turkey, then in France and Norway, and ultimately, at the beginning of 1937, in Mexico.

Trotsky and his wife, Natalie, were housed in a comfortable villa called the Blue House in the Coyoacan suburb of Mexico City. It belonged to the painter Diego Rivera, a founding member of the Mexican Communist Party. During Trotsky's first months there, Stalin staged a show trial in his absence, levying numerous ridiculous charges against the veteran Bolshevik. One was that he had entered into a secret agreement with Rudolf Hess, Adolf Hitler's deputy, offering to cede the whole of the Ukraine to Germany in return for German support for his own return to power in the Soviet Union.

ARMED MEN BURST INTO THE VILLA

In February, 1938, Trotsky's son, Lyova, who had been carrying out intensive research in Paris on Trotsky's behalf, went into a coma and died. He was 32 years old and in

good health. There was no doubt that he had been poisoned. The long arm of the GPU, Stalin's hated and feared secret police, was at work.

Trotsky was then writing a life of Stalin, an uncompromising account, dedicated to showing the Russian dictator in a true light – as a monster. He knew that he had embarked on a dangerous course. He had left the Blue House and moved to a more secure villa, which had been turned into a fortress with bodyguards and machine guns. He kept a revolver in his desk at all times.

Sometime early in 1940, Stalin decided to kill him.

A Narrow Escape

At 4 am on 24 May, 1940, the inmates of the villa were asleep. Apart from Trotsky and Natalie, the villa was occupied by their grandson, Seva, and Alfred and Marguerite Rosmer, friends since the days in France. The guards were quartered some distance from the main building.

Suddenly, armed men burst into the villa.

ABOVE
Trotsky haranguing Red Army troops in 1925. By this time, following the death of Lenin and the rise to power of Stalin, Trotsky's star had begun to wane. He and his family were forced to flee into exile.

They raked the rooms with sub-machine guns and hurled grenades and petrol bombs. Outside, gunfire kept the guards pinned down in their outhouses. Miraculously, no one was badly hurt; the most serious injury was to Seva, who had been hit in the foot. Trtsky and Natalie had been grazed by bullets, but their wounds turned out to be mere scratches.

Later, a police search turned up a three-pound dynamite bomb, fitted with a time fuse which had failed to detonate.

One of the guards, a 25-year-old American named Robert Sheldon Harte, was missing. His body was found later in an abandoned farmhouse in the hills. He had been shot in the head and in the nape of the neck; it was the classic GPU murder method.

ABOVE
Trotsky's study in his villa at Sukham-Kale on the Black Sea in the Caucasus, where he was undergoing treatment for ill-health. At this time he was in daily dread of assassination and was constantly guarded by soldiers. A copy of the *New York American* can be seen on the table.

LEON TROTSKY AND WIFE ARRIVE IN MEXICO CITY, THEY WERE SURROUNDED BY PLAIN CLOTHESMEN AND POLICE.

Investigations revealed that the farmhouse where Harte's body was discovered had been taken over by two brothers, Leopoldo and Luis Arenal, both members of the Mexican Communist Party, a few days before the attack on Trotsky. The farmhouse, in fact, belonged to the painter David Siqueiros, who was married to the Arenals' sister, Angelica. Like Diego Rivera, he was a founder-member of the Mexican Communist Party; in stark contrast to Rivera, he was fanatically pro-Stalin.

Robert Sheldon Harte had been on sentry duty on the night of the attack, and there was evidence that his carelessness had allowed the raiders to enter the grounds of the villa. There was even a suspicion that he had been in league with them. But, as Trotsky's biographer, Robert Payne, points out, Harte was "demonstrably careless but he was not a traitor". Trotsky "refused to listen to anyone who cast any suspicion on him, and whenever his name was mentioned, Trotsky had to fight back his tears". In the garden of his house he set up a bronze plaque with the following blunt inscription: "In Memory of Robert Sheldon Harte, 1915–1940. Murdered by Stalin".

ABOVE LEFT
Trotsky and his wife arrive in Mexico City at the beginning of 1927, heavily guarded by police. They were accommodated in a villa called the Blue House belonging to the painter Diego Rivera, a founder of the Mexican Communist Party.

Knowing that another attack was imminent, Trotsky strengthened the villa's defences. What he did not know was that the enemy was already within.

One of Trotsky's secretarial assistants was a young woman named Sylvia Ageloff. She was regularly driven to the villa by a handsome, charming young man who, judging by his limousine, was well-to-do. He became acquainted with the Rosmers and with Trotsky's grandson, Seva, for whom he bought a model glider.

MORNARD'S FACE HAD A GREY-GREEN HUE

To Sylvia he was Jacques Mornard, a Belgian citizen. His passport said that he was Frank Jacson, a naturalized Canadian citizen who had been born in Yugoslavia; under another assumed identity he was Jacson-Mornard Vandendreschd, the son of a Belgian diplomat.

His real name was Jaime Ramon Mercader del Rio. He was born in Barcelona in 1913 and raised in Paris, where his mother was the mistress of several leading members of the French Communist Party. He was an agent of the GPU.

Trotsky met Mornard on 28 May, 1940. He had given the Rosmers a lift to Vera Cruz, where they were to catch a ship for France, and Natalie had gone along to see them off. Back at the villa, she and Trotsky entertained Mornard with a cup of coffee. The guards became accustomed to the sight of his parking the car outside, then wandering through the gates and spending some time in the garden while he waited for Sylvia to finish work. Sometimes he would chat to Trotsky while the latter fed his pet rabbits.

The Killer Within

Trotsky was with his rabbits when Mornard arrived at the villa on 20 August, 1940. It was a hot afternoon, and it seemed strange that the visitor was carrying a heavy overcoat; Natalie commented on it, when Mornard asked for a glass of water. "It won't last long," was his reply. "It might rain." She noticed that he looked ill; his face had a grey-green hue.

In the lining of the overcoat Mornard had concealed a dagger, a short-handled ice-pick and a revolver. His pallor was due to fear.

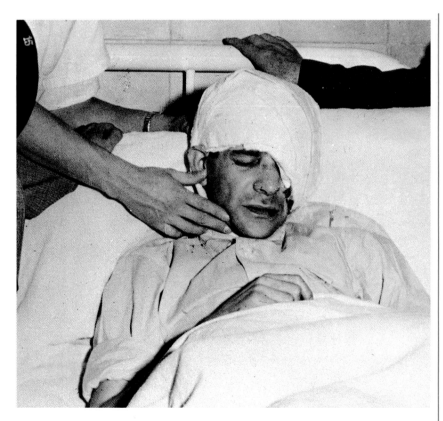

ABOVE
Jacques Mornard, Trotsky's assassin, seen bandaged in hospital after having been severely beaten by Trotsky's bodyguards. His real name was Jaime Ramon Mercader del Rio, and he was born in Barcelona in 1913. He later moved to Paris with his mother.

ABOVE
"Jacques Mornard" snapped by surprise on the patio of the Mexico City prison cell when he had spent ten years of the sentence passed on him for Trotsky's murder. The private cell was paid for through his attorney. He never revealed who, if anyone, had backed him in the killing.

RIGHT
Leon Trotsky seen with his wife Natalie while working on his book on the life of Stalin. It was an uncompromising account, dedicated to showing the Russian dictator in his true light. The knowledge that it was being written probably cost Trotsky his life.

Mornard spent a few minutes talking with Trotsky by the rabbit hutches. He had brought the manuscript of an article for Trotsky to read. Trotsky invited him into his study.

Mornard had been in the room before and knew what measures existed for Trotsky's self-protection. Under the writing-table there was a switch to activate an alarm system; in a drawer there was a Colt .38 automatic; and on the table itself, serving as a paperweight, there lay a small .25 automatic. Both weapons were loaded.

As Trotsky sat down, Mornard arranged his overcoat on the table top so that it would be hard for Trotsky to reach the alarm switch quickly. He sat on the edge of the table, looking down at Trotsky's bare head, with its thinning white hair. Slowly he reached inside his overcoat and brought out the ice-pick. He raised it and, closing his eyes, brought it down with full force on Trotsky's skull.

But Mornard had made a mistake. He had intended to strike Trotsky with the needle-sharp pointed end of the pick, driving it four or five inches into the victim's brain and killing him instantly. Instead, the impact was made by the flattened end, and the slightly curved, two-inch-wide blade made a wound only about two and a half inches deep. Trotsky's major reflexes remained unimpaired. Rising from his chair, he hurled himself on his assailant with extraordinary strength and bit his hand deeply. He let out a terrible scream.

Natalie heard the scream and came rushing into the room. She saw her husband standing there, blood pouring down his face, and rushed to his side. He swayed and slumped to the floor. It was only then that she saw Mornard, his face contorted with fear, gasping for breath. She rushed over to grapple with him.

Guards who had heard Trotsky's scream, burst into the study. They hurled Mornard to the floor and beat him severely. Meanwhile, Trotsky had somehow managed to

TROTSKY HURLED HIMSELF ON HIS ASSAILANT

get up. He staggered on to the balcony and down the steps to the patio, where he again collapsed. Natalie placed a pillow under his head, wiped the blood from his face and tried to soothe the wound with ice. She did not yet know the serious nature of his wound; it looked quite superficial.

An ambulance arrived and took the injured man to hospital, where surgeons performed an opperation to remove four square inches of his skull. Their efforts were in vain.

Trotsky had been in a coma when he arrived at the hospital and he died at 7.25 pm the next day.

His murderer was subjected to months of interrogations and psychiatric examinations; they revealed nothing, except that he was a pathological liar. He stood on trial in the spring of 1943, was convicted of Trotsky's murder and sentenced to 20 years in prison.

It was not until September, 1950, that the police discovered Mornard's true identity. A hardened Communist, he had become a political commissar with the rank of lieutenant in the Republican Army's 27th Division during the Spanish Civil War, and was recruited into Soviet intelligence. After the defeat of the Republican Army he had gone to the Soviet Union, where he received training in a GPU school. His mother, Caridad del Rio, became the mistress of the man who had recruited him, General Kotov.

On 6 May, 1960, Ramon Mercader walked free. Accompanied by two guards from the Czechoslovak Embassy in Mexico City, and bearing a diplomatic passport under the name Jacques Vandendreschd, he boarded a Cuban airliner and flew to Havana, where he stopped for only a few hours before flying on to Prague. Nothing more was ever heard of him.

ABOVE
Trotsky's heavily fortified house in Mexico City. Its high walls and machine gun posts did not prevent an attack with sub-machine guns, petrol bombs and grenades by would-be assassins on 24 May, 1940. Trotsky and Natalie were both slightly wounded.

DALLAS, 1963: WHO KILLED KENNEDY?

Three years after Mercader was freed, President John F. Kennedy died, his head blown apart by an assassin's bullet on 22 November, 1963. Speculation about who that assassin really was, and what organization, if any, was behind his action, has run to millions of words, featured in a dozen TV documentaries and a recent film.

The "accepted" version, the conclusion of the Warren Commission – which carried out the first official inquiry into the assassination – was that President Kennedy was murdered by one man, Lee Harvey Oswald, who had lain in wait with a sniper's rifle in the window of a warehouse overlooking Dealey Plaza and killed his victim with two gunshots, one through the throat, the other in the head.

Oswald was 24 years old; a Russian linguist, he had served as a radar operator in the US Marine Corps at Atsugi, in Japan, one of the bases from which Lockheed U-2 reconnaissance aircraft took off on their clandestine flights over the Soviet Union. In 1959 he defected to the USSR, but later

ABOVE
This photograph, taken ten years after the assassination, shows the building which housed the Texas School Book Depository. It was from here that Lee Harvey Oswald allegedly fired the fatal shots.

The recording indicated not three shots, but four

returned to the United States, where he dabbled in Cuban revolutionary politics.

The lasting image of Oswald is that he was a left-wing malcontent, but his true character remains a mystery. He had no apparent motive for killing President Kennedy and, if there was a motive, it will never be known. Oswald was himself gunned down on 24 November, 1963, two days after his arrest. His killer was Jack Ruby, a local nightclub owner with Mafia connections, who shot Oswald as the latter was being escorted to Dallas county jail.

The majority of Americans initially accepted the official explanation of Oswald's guilt, but there were some who did not, and their dissatisfaction eventually spread to Congress, which in 1976 voted to conduct its own investigation into both President Kennedy's death and that of the civil rights

leader, Martin Luther King, who was murdered in 1968. The House Assassinations Committee was formed for the purpose.

The Committee's first chairman told the House in 1978 that he was convinced that President Kennedy had been the victim of a conspiracy, and within weeks there came a clear indication that the Kennedy case was not all it seemed.

An acoustics specialist, brought in to analyse a recording made on the day of the assassination, concluded that the recording indicated not three shots, as had originally been thought, but four. He concluded that it would have been physically impossible for Oswald to have fired four shots in the time available. Also, the report of one shot was louder than the others and seemed to have come from a different direction.

LEFT
Seconds after the assassin's bullet slammed into President Kennedy's head, Secret Service agent Clinton Hill dives to the

assistance of Jacqueline Kennedy. Rising from her seat in panic and terror, she might have fallen from the speeding vehicle had it not been for his prompt action.

RIGHT
Detective J. C. Day of the Dallas Police Department holds up the bolt-action rifle with telescopic sights that was claimed to be the murder weapon. It led straight to Oswald's arrest – but was Oswald's finger on the trigger on the day of the assassination?

In the summer of 1979, after further scientific investigation, the Assassinations Committee disclosed that President Kennedy "was probably assassinated as the result of a conspiracy". The Committee expressed no doubt that it was Oswald's bullet that had actually killed the President; the implication was that he had been the tool of a well-organized undercover group like the Mafia or anti-Castro activists, both of whom had motives for wanting Kennedy dead. The Committee singled out two leading Mafia bosses, Carlos Marcello and Santos Trafficante, and investigative work revealed that both Oswald and his killer, Jack Ruby, had had connections, albeit tenuous, with Marcello's organization.

THE FILE STAYS OPEN

Nevertheless, there were a number of loopholes in the Committee's argument. Suggestions that the Central Intelligence Agency or the Federal Bureau of Investigation might have been involved in the murder were dismissed, even though the Committee had earlier concluded that key evidence had been deliberately destroyed by FBI officials. The Committee failed to investigate fully reports

BELOW
This diagram shows the sequence of events as they were thought to have unfolded on that fateful day of 22 November, 1963. The motorcade route is clearly marked, as is the room in the Book Depository from where Lee Harvey Oswald is said to have fired. But what about clear eye-witness accounts of other concealed marksmen involved in the killing?

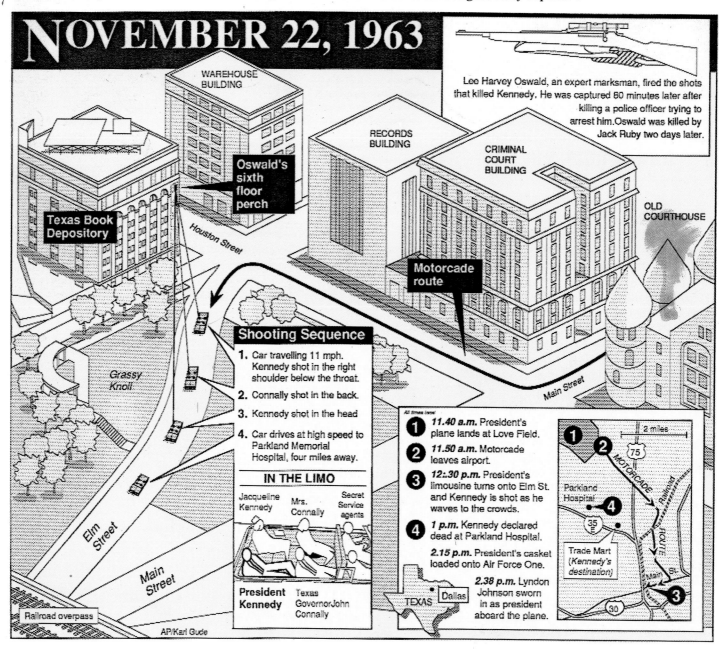

NOVEMBER 22, 1963

Lee Harvey Oswald, an expert marksman, fired the shots that killed Kennedy. He was captured 80 minutes later after killing a police officer trying to arrest him. Oswald was killed by Jack Ruby two days later.

WAREHOUSE BUILDING

RECORDS BUILDING

CRIMINAL COURT BUILDING

OLD COURTHOUSE

Oswald's sixth floor perch

Texas Book Depository

Houston Street

Motorcade route

Grassy Knoll

Elm Street

Main Street

Shooting Sequence

1. Car travelling 11 mph. Kennedy shot in the right shoulder below the throat.
2. Connally shot in the back.
3. Kennedy shot in the head
4. Car drives at high speed to Parkland Memorial Hospital, four miles away.

IN THE LIMO

Jacqueline Kennedy — Mrs. Connally — Secret Service agents

President Kennedy — Texas Governor John Connally

All times local

① **11.40 a.m.** President's plane lands at Love Field.

② **11.50 a.m.** Motorcade leaves airport.

③ **12:.30 p.m.** President's limousine turns onto Elm St. and Kennedy is shot as he waves to the crowds.

④ **1 p.m.** Kennedy declared dead at Parkland Hospital.

2.15 p.m. President's casket loaded onto Air Force One.

2.38 p.m. Lyndon Johnson sworn in as president aboard the plane.

Main Street

Railroad overpass

AP/Karl Gude

2 miles

75

Parkland Hospital

35

Trade Mart (Kennedy's destination)

MOTORCADE ROUTE

Railroad

Main St.

TEXAS · Dallas

30

that Oswald had been reported in the company of right-wing FBI agents and that he had links with the CIA. There was another matter, too, that never received in-depth appraisal – the fact that several of the Mafia men suspected of involvement with the Kennedy assassination had secretly been plotting with the CIA to murder the Cuban President, Fidel Castro.

Out of the mass of material that has emerged from various investigations into the murder of President Kennedy, three distinct groups may be targeted for possible complicity: the Mafia, the US Intelligence services and the anti-Castro activists. In March, 1979, the Assassinations Committee asked the Department of Justic to arrange specialist examination of all the films shot on that fateful day in Dealey Plaza, to study the acoustics evidence, to review the Com-

mittee's findings, and to report whether further investigation was justified. It took nearly 10 years for the Department to produce its findings. In March, 1988, in a five-page report to Congress, it concluded that "no persuasive evidence can be identified to support the theory of a conspiracy" in the assassination of either President Kennedy or Martin Luther King. "No further investigation appears to be warranted unless new information, sufficient to support additional investigative activity, becomes available."

The media have repeatedly tried to place such information before the American public, only to see their efforts broken again and again by officialdom. But someone, somewhere, knows the truth, and even after three decades the world is eager to learn it.

The file on the murder of President Kennedy remains open.

ABOVE
This is an accurate reconstruction of the killing of Lee Harvey Oswald by Jack Ruby, a local nightclub owner with Mafia connections. Oswald was shot on 24 November, 1963, two days after his arrest, as he was being escorted to Dallas County Jail.

THE UGLY HISTORY OF POLITICAL MURDER

The name assassin comes from a fanatical 12th-century Muslim sect in Iran that developed organized political murder as a method of unifying the Islamic world. The leader of this sect was Hasan ibn-al-Sabah, known as "The Old Man of the Mountain". He is said to have created a beautiful garden, full of lush fruits and beautiful women. Volunteers were drugged with hashish – giving the sect its name of Hashashins, or assassins – and taken to the garden. They were allowed to indulge all their worldly desires there. This was a taste of the paradise that awaited anyone who died in Hasan's service. Since this reward did not depend on the success of the mission, they fought fanatically, without fear.

Organized groups of political assassins gained prominence in the late 19th century. In 1881 a group called *Narodnaya Volya* – "the People's Will" – assassinated Tsar Alexander II. A similar group in Serbia, called *Narodna Obrana* – "National Defence" – sought to free the Serbs from the Austro-Hungarian Empire. Its assassination squad, known as the "Black Hand", was responsible for killing Archduke Ferdinand and his wife at Sarajevo, thus sparking off the First World War.

Four American presidents have died at the hands of assassins – Abraham Lincoln, James Garfield, William McKinley and John F. Kennedy. And unsuccessful attempts were made on the lives of Andrew Jackson, Theodore Roosevelt, Gerald Ford and Ronald Reagan.

Only one British prime minister, Spencer Percival, has been assassinated. He was shot by John Bellingham in the lobby of the House of Commons in 1812. An attempt was made on Sir Robert Peel in 1843, but the assassin, Daniel M'Naghten, killed Peel's secretary by mistake.

LEFT
President Kennedy's flag-draped coffin on its last journey to Arlington Cemetery. Beside it, veiled in black, can be seen Jacqueline; she is flanked by the late President's brothers Edward and Robert, who was himself to die at the hands of an assassin.

INDEX

Herald *Tribune*

KENNEDY ASSA

s Shot Down in Car by a
s He Rides Through D
ohnson Qu

NEW YORK POS

CAUGH

MILWAUKEE COUNTY
SHERIFF'S DEPARTMENT
5 6 5 8 0 · 8 · 08 · 82

PICTURE CREDITS

T = top; B = bottom; L = left; R = right

AP/Wide World Photos: pages 2 (& 40), 6, 7, 8, 8–9, 9, 10, 11, 12, 13, 14, 15, 16, 17T, 17BL, 18, 19, 22B, 23, 24, 25, 26, 27B, 28, 29, 30, 31R, 32, 35, 36, 37T, 39, 43, 44, 44–5, 45, 46B, 46–7, 47, 59L, 60TR, 65, 69B, 70, 71, 72T. John Frost Historical Newspaper Services: pages 17BR, 42, 47, 56T, 58, 59R, 60TL, 69T. The Hulton-Deutsch Collection: pages 20 (& 31L), 21, 22T, 27T, 33, 34 (& 48R), 49, 50T, 52B, 53, 54 (& 57B), 55, 56B, 57T, 60B, 62B, 63, 64T, 66, 68, 76–7. Robert Jackson: pages 37B, 38, 41L, 46L, 48L, 51, 62T, 64B, 72, 74, 75. Robert Jackson and AP/Wirephoto: pages 52T, 73B. Robert Jackson and the Press Association: pages 50B, 52BR. Robert Jackson and the Varley Picture Agency: page 41R. The Mansell Collection: pages 61, 67.